I CAN'T DO IT ANY MORE
AND I'M NOT SATISFIED

——Are you fed up with your parents?

——Is a friend of yours threatening to commit suicide?

——Are you having problems with drugs or alcohol?

——Ever wonder what's the point of being alive anyhow?

——Do you feel lonely, cut off, misunderstood?

Author Joyce Vedral's been there and back. And in this book she'll show you how to cope with—and even overcome—the difficulties, pressures, and frustrations in your life.

**THE WORLD DOESN'T CHANGE. *WE DO.*
START TODAY.**

JOYCE L. VEDRAL, Ph.D.

I CAN'T TAKE IT ANY MORE

How To Get Up When You're Really Low

BALLANTINE BOOKS • NEW YORK

To everyone who has ever said or thought, "I can't take it any more."

Library of Congress Catalog Card Number: 87-91475

ISBN 0-345-33979-7

Printed in Canada

First Edition: September 1987
Third Printing: March 1990

– ACKNOWLEDGMENTS –

Thank you Marthe Simone Vedral, Jennifer Berkowitz, and Allison Limer for your careful reading and constructive criticism of the manuscript.

Special thanks to the ninth grade students in Ms. James Perine's English classes at Halsey Junior High School for sharing your thoughts and feelings with me.

Thank you Jason Vale for your deep insights concerning issues raised in this book.

Thank you Marilyn Abraham for initiating this project.

Thank you Bob Wyatt for your brilliant and cheerful editing.

Thank you Beth Rashbaum for your sensitive fine-tuning of the manuscript.

Thank you Andrea Laine and Liz Williams for your relentless enthusiasm in working with this project and with me.

Thank you Richard McCoy for your kind assistance.

Deep love and appreciation goes to my mother, Martha Yellin, for being there now, in my adult years, when I still need her.

Thank you Dave Yellin, my wonderful father, for teaching me how to sublimate my energy in positive directions.

Thank you friends and family for your continual interest and encouragement.

Special thanks to my agent, Rick Balkin, for continual faith in my projects.

– TABLE OF CONTENTS –

1

Why Am I Here? How to Find a Reason for Living

Do you ever feel hopeless and helpless about the direction of your life? Do you wonder why you're here? If you do, welcome to the club. Most people feel that way from time to time.

The question "What is the meaning of life?" has plagued every one of us. People have come up with a variety of unsatisfactory answers. "Life is for pleasure—to see how much fun you can have, as long as you don't hurt anyone." "Life is to work hard in order to survive." It's full of pain, and suffering. We will get our reward in the afterlife."

If that's all life has to offer, I would have bowed out a long time ago.

Dr. Sol Gordon says: "Life is not a meaning, it's an opportunity."[1] Yes. An opportunity to use your potential.

---

[1]Dr. Sol Gordon, *When Living Hurts* (New York: Union of American Hebrew Congregations, 1985), p. 12.

Each person has potential, and each person is challenged to use that potential to the greatest possible degree.

We all have a different amount and kind of potential. It's not your job to measure up to my potential and it's not my job to measure up to yours. All you have to do is to make the most of what you were given. There's an interesting parable (a story told to teach a truth about life) which illustrates this point exactly. Jesus was talking to some people about what a person must do in this life in order to be happy and to please God. Jesus told the story

. . . of a man going into another country, who called together his servants and loaned them money to invest for him while he was gone. He gave $5,000 to one, $2,000 to another, and $1,000 to the last—dividing it in proportion to their abilities—and then left on his trip. The man who received the $5,000 began immediately to buy and sell with it and soon earned another $5,000. The man with $2,000 went right to work too, and earned another $2,000. But the man who received $1,000 dug a hole in the ground and hid the money for safekeeping. After a long time the master returned from his trip and called them to him to account for his money. The man to whom he had entrusted $5,000 brought him $10,000. His master praised him for his good work. "You have been faithful in handling this small amount," he told him, "so now I will give you many more responsibilities. Begin the joyous tasks I have assigned to you. Next came the man who had received the $2,000, with the report, "Sir, you gave me $2,000 to use, and I have doubled it." "Good work," his master said. "You are a good and faithful servant. You have been faithful over this small amount. Now I will give you much more." Then the man with the $1,000 came and said, "Sir, I knew you were a hard man, and I was afraid. . . . so I hid your money in the earth and here it is!" But the master replied, "Wicked man! Lazy slave! Since you knew I would demand a profit, you should at least have put my money in the bank so I could have some interest. Take the money from this man and give it to the man with the $10,000. *For the man who uses well what he is given shall be given more. . . . But from the man who is unfaithful, even what little responsibility he has shall be taken from him.* And throw the useless servant into outer darkness: There shall be weeping and gnashing of teeth.[2]

We are responsible to make the most of the talent that has been given us. If we do not, the talent we do have will go to waste—will be taken away from us. In other words, "use it or lose it." If we are afraid, as was the man who was given the $1,000, and if we bury or hide our talent, not only will we eventually lose that talent, but we will spend our later years regretting having wasted our lives. But if we use our talents, like the two men who doubled their money, we will increase what we already have and be generously rewarded for our efforts.

Your job is clear. You must find out what your potential is and use that potential to the best of your ability. In other words, discover your purpose in life—what psychologist Dr. George Weinberg calls your job: "We must define our 'job' in life. . . . In the end we can ask ourselves, have we done this job?"[3]

[2]Matthew 25:14–30.

[3]Dr. George Weinberg, *Self Creation* (New York: St. Martin's Press, 1978), p.82

– FINDING YOUR JOB
(PURPOSE) IN LIFE –

All well and good. "We must define our job in life."
Lovely words. But how do we do that? The first step is so
simple that at first you might believe it's too easy to work.
It's right there in front of you. Think about what you really
like to do. What do you get a kick out of? Do you enjoy
being argumentative—proving a point? Are you a whiz at
organizing people—always the leader when it comes to
setting up parties, trips, etc.? Are you a natural diplomat
who can settle arguments and get people to cooperate? If
you're argumentative and enjoy proving a point, your job
in life might be to become a lawyer. If you are good at
organizing, perhaps you should get involved in politics or
administration. If you're a natural diplomat, you might
want to do people-oriented work, perhaps as a psychologist
or teacher. Look to your likes to find your "destiny."

To narrow the field still further, let's look at what you
hate. Do you hate listening to people's problems? Are you
horrified at the prospect of working with numbers? Then
you certainly know that you're not going to be a psychologist or an accountant. Think this through carefully. I have a
friend who started an adoption service because she loved
kids and wanted to do something for them. But she hated
working with grown-ups, listening to them talk about
themselves and their problems—which of course as an
adoption counselor was her major responsibility. She
laughs at herself now, but she had an unhappy couple of
years before she understood that she'd picked the wrong
career.

Stop and think. Make a list of things you enjoy and
another of things you hate.

THINGS I ENJOY	THINGS I HATE
1.	1.
2.	2.
3.	3.
4.	4.
5.	5.

Look at your lists. Once you come to terms with what you honestly love and hate, you narrow your field of choices considerably. Looking back at my own life, it's easy to see now why I would become a teacher and a writer. I used to love to explain things to friends. I loved learning new words and I loved to read. Yet I missed the obvious. Instead of asking myself what I honestly liked and disliked, I became a secretary. I found myself doing something I hated—taking dictation, writing other people's letters. Why did I do this? I followed in my older sister's footsteps. I listened to people who said: "Why go to school all those years when a secretary makes more than a teacher?" Because I ignored my own inner voice I ended up hating to get up on Monday mornings to face the week in front of me. Fortunately, I soon came to my senses and realized I could not spend the rest of my life doing something I hated. I went back to college and eventually became an English teacher and a writer, and even though my sister was making more than I was (by then she had been promoted to the position of "executive secretary") I didn't care because now I couldn't wait to get up on Monday mornings. In fact, I used to laugh when I'd pick up my paycheck. It seemed strange to get paid for having so much fun. I really loved what I was doing.

You know what else? If you don't love your work you'll probably never really be good at it. My sister was promoted to the top because she loved her work. I would have been lucky if they didn't fire me (and as I recall now, there was some talk of that going around the office).

Instead of wasting a lot of time trying to fool yourself, and then having to backtrack to make things right, be honest with yourself from the beginning. If a job idea doesn't excite you, doesn't send a spark flying, it's probably not what you're meant to spend the best years of your life doing—even if it's what you think you should be doing.

The second way to find out what you really should do with your life is to ask yourself, "What would I like to do with my life, if I weren't afraid I wouldn't be good enough to do it, or worried that it would take too many years of school, or frightened off by the competition?" What do you spend a lot of mental time "fighting down," giving yourself excuses for not trying? That is probably the very thing you really want to do. Looking back, I can remember that I would think about being an English teacher, and then I would quickly counter with the thought: "No, you would never have the time to read all those books; besides, you're not intellectual enough—English teachers are more intelligent than you are."

Think of your own wildest dreams. What would you really love to be but are scared to admit even to yourself? Write it here. You may have a few ideas.

WHAT I WISH I COULD BE
1.
2.
3.

Another way to find out what you should do with your life is to take into account what you're always getting complimented on. What do your teachers and parents say you're special in? Have you heard over the years: "You should be an actress," or "You'd be some lawyer," or "I wish my doctor was like you." Write the list here.

PEOPLE HAVE SAID I'D BE A GREAT

1.
2.
3.

Now look at all three lists: what you love and hate doing, what you've always dreamed of doing but are afraid to dare to try, and what people have always said you'd be great at. These are clues to what you are destined to do with the rest of your life.

These three considerations will eventually develop into what is called an "inner voice," telling you what you really should do with your life. Dr. Irene Kassorla, psychologist and author, says,

> Everyone has a secret desire. It is an inner voice tell-
> ing you what you can do. I think an awful lot of
> people think their secret desire is too good for them.
> Too fanciful. They are worried that they can't do it.[4]

Now that you have an idea about what you should do with your life, take the next step and assume the responsibility for becoming the person who can do it. No one else can do it for you. Only you can create your destiny. As much as your family and friends love you, they cannot hear your inner voice.

Listening to that inner voice will give you a goal. And, believe it or not, just having a goal can put you on a natural high. It has been discovered that when you have a goal that

[4]Dr. Irene Kassorla, *Go For It!* (New York: Dell Publishing Co., 1984), p. 117.

you believe in and are working toward, your body releases chemicals called "endorphins." These hormones are actually similar to morphine, but with no harmful effects. They produce a happy feeling and block out negative feelings and pain.[5] Haven't you ever met someone who seems to be on a natural high?

But there's a catch. In order to be really happy, in order to be really successful in the long run, you have to make sure your goals involve helping people. Studies have been done on the most financially successful people, and it has been discovered that those who make it big are those who genuinely try to help people who are in need of something, whether it be a product, health care, advice, etc. It really isn't that mysterious when you think about it. If you offer people a product or service that they need, they will be happy to pay you for it. Whether you're a doctor, a salesman, a beautician, or a carpenter, if you offer people a valuable service, with the goal of really helping them, eventually you will be successful. If your goal, however, is to rip people off, you may become successful and wealthy for a short time, but eventually you will be found out and you're likely to end up poor.

Aside from financial considerations, think of this. Who are the people whom the world really honors? Is it those who lived only to please themselves? No. We forget about them. Psychologist Alfred Adler put it beautifully:

> If we look around us today at the heritage we have received from our ancestors, what do we see? All that survives of them is the contribution they made to human life. We see cultivated ground, we see roadways and buildings. . . . These results have been left by men who contributed to human welfare. What has

[5]Dennis Waitley, *Seeds of Greatness, The Ten Best Kept Secrets of Total Success* (New Jersey: The Fleming H. Revell Co., 1983), p. 154.

happened to the others . . . who asked only "What can I get out of life?" They have left no trace behind them. Not only are they dead; their whole lives were futile. It is as if our earth itself has spoken to them and said, "We don't need you, you are not fitted for life. There is no future for your aims and strivings. . . . Be off with you. You are not wanted. Die and disappear.[6]

Now that you've given your purpose in life some careful thought, it's time to start setting specific goals. Without a goal you drift—you wander aimlessly. When you leave your house in the morning you don't go outside until you have decided where you are going. Otherwise you would just walk around in a confused state. It's the same way in life. You must have a specific goal if you expect to get anywhere. Most people who wonder why they didn't achieve success in life probably never really set a goal. Napoleon Hill, author of the book *Think and Grow Rich*, says,

Examine the first hundred people you meet. Ask them what they want most in life, and ninety-eight of them will not be able to tell you. . . . Riches do not respond to wishes. They respond only to definite plans, backed by definite desires, through constant persistence.[7]

[6]Alfred Adler, *What Life Should Mean to You*, Alan Porter, ed. (New York: G.P. Putnam's Sons, Perigree Books Inc., 1931), pp. 10–11.

[7]Napoleon Hill, *Think and Grow Rich* (New York: Fawcett Crest Publishing Co., 1960), p. 162.

– USING YOUR SUBCONSCIOUS MIND TO HELP YOU REACH A GOAL –

Once you know what you hope to do with your life, write it down. For example, suppose you dare to believe that some day you'll be a professional baseball, basketball, tennis, or hockey player. You might even dream of becoming well-known. Write down a phrase such as "Star Player." Now take three small business-size cards and write the key phrase on each one of them. Next place the cards in three different places where your eye will catch them when you're off guard. This way the words can go into your subconscious mind time and again. You might decide to place one in a dresser drawer that you open every morning, another on a subject divider in your notebook that you see every afternoon, and the third in your closet where you hang up your clothes in the evening. The idea is to allow your subconscious mind to absorb your dream and to register it as reality.[8]

Your subconscious mind acts like a guided missile which has been programmed to reach a specific target. Although the guided missile doesn't usually travel in a direct line—it zigzags around obstacles—it always "remembers" the goal and eventually reaches the target. When you program your subconscious mind to reach a goal it may have to do some zig-zagging to get you around the setbacks that come your way, but eventually it will make sure you reach your goal. The cards help to program your subconscious. I've used them and they really do work—in combination with other things which I will also talk about.

Programming your subconscious mind is important, but

---

[8]Claude M. Bristol, *The Magic of Believing* (New York: Simon & Schuster, Pocket Books, 1948), p. 86. I got the idea of using these cards from this book.

that's not enough. You must take practical steps to develop your goal into a specific plan. That will require setting a lot of intermediate goals.

– THE IMPORTANCE OF
MAKING PLANS –

Lee Iacocca, business magnate and president of General Motors, says, "Whenever one of my people has an idea, I ask him to lay it out in writing."[9] Write your ultimate goal on a piece of paper and under it write the steps that will be necessary to achieve that goal. For example, suppose you want to be a professional baseball player. Right now you are a sophomore in high school. The plan might look like this.

Goal: Professional Baseball player
Plan: 1. Get good marks in all academic subjects to fulfill the school requirement for getting on the high school team.
2. Begin a physical fitness program of daily running to build up stamina.
3. Join the high school baseball team.
4. Put the best effort into games and become known as a top player.
5. Ask the coach to set up "tryouts" for pro teams.
6. Make one of the training camps for a pro team. Be a star pro player by the age of 23.

[9]Lee Iacocca, (with William Novak), *Iacocca* (New York: Bantam Books, 1984), p. 43.

Does this sound farfetched? Well it isn't. By making your goal into a plan, you're giving your subconscious mind more material to work with. Even just writing it down will make it more likely that you will actually take steps. In the above example, having written down "Speak to the baseball coach about how to become a pro," you would find yourself blurting out one day to the coach, "What's involved in becoming a pro?" You would do that because your subconscious mind would count it as unfinished business and keep reminding you to do it. The long-range plan can be written out for whatever your goal is—musician, doctor, lawyer, actor, top executive—anything. Write your plan and your goal here.

Goal:

Plan: 1.

2.

3.

4.

5.

6.

7.

8.

9.

10.

Another thing you can do to help you reach your goal in life is to talk to people who are already successful in that field. For example, if you're interested in becoming a doctor, talk to your family doctor, or call your local hospital and ask for their public relations department. Tell them you're interested in talking to some interns (student doctors).

Go to the library. Most librarians are delighted to help young people who are genuinely interested in seeking information. They'll help you to get all kinds of books related to your field.

Then check some paperback bookstores. The clerk will direct you to the section where books dealing with your field of interest are located. The advantage of buying the books is twofold. First, you can underline information and keep the book, and second you may find more up-to-date books in the bookstore than in the library.

While you're doing all this reading, don't forget one of the most important things. Read biographies and autobiographies—the stories of people who made it. If you're interested in becoming a musician, read the life stories of stars whom you admire. There are books on most of them —Michael Jackson, Diana Ross, Prince, Bruce Springsteen, and more recent artists as well. Whatever your field, there exists a biography or autobiography of someone who made it. You can pick up clues from such books and you can get inspired, too.

Now that you've set your goals and made specific plans and done some research, something strange starts to occur. Out of the clear blue sky, "luck" or coincidence seems to help you fulfill your goal. What is this strange phenomenon?

– SYNCHRONICITY, SERENDIPITY, OR GOOD LUCK? –

Synchronicity is a phrase coined by psychologist Carl G. Jung. He was fascinated by the fact that many of his patients, when pursuing a goal, would happen into experiences which seemed like coincidence, but were connected so meaningfully to other events in their lives, that they could not have been just good luck. Jung came up with the idea that it must be the unconscious that draws these seemingly "lucky" events into the life of the "lucky" individual.[10] It appears that our unconscious energy sees to it that we are "in the right place at the right time." But all of this only occurs if we have set our will, our conscious mind, on achieving a worthy goal.

Carl Jung talks about a patient he had who was trying to achieve mental health. Jung was in the process of attempting to convince the woman that the phenomenon of synchronicity exists. One night the woman had a dream, and in the dream she saw a rare beetle, a "Golden Scarab." The next day she was in a therapy session with Jung and in the process of describing the dream. At that moment there was a strange scratching on the screen of the window, which became so annoying Jung had to stop the session to check it out. He opened the window, and there on the screen was a Golden Scarab beetle, which was almost never seen in that part of the world. Needless to say, the patient was convinced that synchronicity exists.[11]

I have had numerous experiences which involve synchronicity. Recently I went to speak to a television producer about being a guest on his show in connection with a book I had written that included short, true stories by teenagers. He was interested in having me appear on the show, but if and only if I could bring at least one of the teenagers with me. Not wanting to lose the deal, I said "Of course I can," all the time knowing that these students had all graduated two years ago and I had no way of contacting any one of them. After I left his office I had other business in

[10]Carl G. Jung, *Synchronicity* (New Jersey: Princeton University press, 1973), p. 21.

[11]Ibid. pp. 21–24.

the city, and since it was a lovely day I decided to walk the fifteen blocks to my next destination, which was five blocks across town and ten blocks uptown. At random I walked across a block and up a couple of blocks, and so on. Suddenly I heard my last name being called, "Vedral." I looked around and finally noticed someone poking his head out of a white Corvette. It was Levon, a former student of mine, and one of the writers of the short stories in the book. Needless to say, I was astounded. I ran over to the car, quickly told him my problem, got his phone number, and made plans to appear with him on the show.

Was it just a coincidence or was there something else in operation—a force which is somehow related to unconscious energy—a force coming from my will which was directed toward my goal?

Dr. Scott M. Peck, psychologist and author of the best-selling book *The Road Less Traveled*, talks about a similar phenomenon. He calls it "serendipity."[12] Serendipity is the gift of finding something valuable or agreeable when you're not looking for it at that particular moment. I had a double experience of serendipity recently. On a morning when I usually run five miles, I decided to jump rope while watching T.V. instead. I turned on the Phil Donahue show. It so happened that Cher was being interviewed. One of the questions Donahue asked her was, "How did you break into movies?" Cher described a "strange coincidence." She talked about how she had made up her mind to rid herself of her 1960s image as part of the Sonny and Cher singing team. She moved to New York enrolled in acting school and began pursuing every possible lead for acting parts. Nothing seemed to be happening. Then one day, Cher's mother called her but accidentally dialed the wrong

[12]Scott M. Peck, M.D., *The Road Less Traveled* (New York: Simon & Schuster, 1978), p. 309.

number. As it turns out, the number she dialed was that of a well-known movie producer who was a longtime acquaintance of hers. "Hello, Cher?" her mother asked. "No. Who is this?" the angry producer barked, having been awakened. Recognizing his voice, Cher's mother apologized. "I'm sorry, I thought I was dialing Cher's number." The producer then got into the conversation with Cher's mother and eventually got around to asking how Cher was doing. Cher's mother mentioned that she was in New York trying to break into serious acting. One thing led to another, and Cher ended up getting a screen test for a part that led to the successful films she's starred in since then.

Cher's serendipity turned out to be mine, too. That day, a day when I usually run and would never ordinarily have turned on the television at that time, I happened to be writing this chapter and was casting about in my mind for current examples of serendipity. So that was a nice bit of luck for me—but was it just luck?

I say no. In my opinion there is a force beyond the power of our intellect to comprehend—a force that operates in our favor when we have directed our will and our energy toward a worthy goal. It seems as if the very universe rises up to help us. For years religious people have explained such forces as "miracles" or "the hand of God." Today, many religious readers as well as psychologists and other experts from various fields recognize that there is a force that assists those in search of a goal. Call it good luck, call it synchronicity, call it serendipity, call it a miracle. It exists. There is that extra help you can expect when you are doing the best you can to achieve your goal.

Perhaps you can think of something that has already happened to you . . . reminds you of what we've been discussing here. If not, be aware of the possibility, and when it happens, accept it as a sign that you are on the right track.

Sometimes a seemingly bad event will happen to you, but that event was necessary in order to cause you to achieve your destiny. This happened to former President Eisenhower. Eisenhower had intended to become a professional football player, but something happened during his college years which forced him to give up football and call contact sports—for life. He suffered a knee injury. Since he ended up becoming one of the best presidents of the United States, it is evident that fate intervened to cause him to take the path that destiny had ordained for him.[13] Think about your own life. Did something bad ever happen to you that in the long run turned out to be a good thing? I believe that if you dedicate yourself to doing the best possible thing with your life, then even if you are mistaken and are pursuing the wrong goal, fate will intervene to help you correct your course.

It's wonderful to feel as if life has something to offer—to believe that you can achieve a great future for yourself. But what do you do about the fact that so many other people in the world are suffering—the bums on the street, the poor, the starving? And what about other threats such as nuclear disaster? Doesn't this make it all a big farce?

– DEALING WITH DEPRESSING THOUGHTS AND REALITIES –

Sixteen-year-old Johanna says,

Watching beggars in the street depresses me. I'm glad I'm not them but it makes me sick to see them and how nobody gives them anything.

[13] Dwight D. Eisenhower, *At Ease* (New York: Doubleday & Company, 1967), p. 15.

But fifteen-year-old Elizabeth says,

I saw a bum begging for money. I hesitated for a moment and started to think about the tragedies that had probably happened to him. He looked really hungry so I took out my two dollars and fifty cents (which was to buy a ticket for the movies) and gave it to him. Then I walked away feeling light, as if I had helped another human being.

You may not be able to save the world, but you can help a little. By giving in to that tug at your heart, you will not only be helping the person you give to, you will be making a dent in the suffering in the world and you will feel better yourself. Which girl walked away happier? The one who did something about her compassion. Elizabeth experienced a "light feeling," or a high, because she had, as she put it, "helped another human being." In short, do what you can when you feel the urge to do it. You may not be able to save the people who just got hit by a volcano on the other side of the world (although you may be able to do something even there) but you certainly can reach out to someone who is right next to you.

Finally, what about the threat of a nuclear disaster? Doesn't that make it all a useless waste of time? Seventeen-year-old Rob says,

What's the use. Sooner or later some nut will press the button and we'll all be blown away.

Nice excuse. Just because the world could end, we should all go on drugs or stop going to school. Let's face it. If there is a nuclear wipeout we'll all be destroyed. Then there will be nothing to worry about, will there? But in the meantime what's to stop you from living right and feeling good about yourself?

If you're going to let that "What if" stop you from living, you might as well add some more imminent (about to happen) "what ifs" to your list. What about cancer? Maybe you'll get that. What if you get hit by a drunk driver? What if you get mugged and murdered? What if your home catches fire in the middle of the night and you are burned to death? Morbid thinking, isn't it? So forget all the what ifs and devote the time that you do have to working on achieving your destiny in life. Life is short, no matter how long you live, so let's get on with the exciting business of living. Let's get with the program.

Saying: *Let's get with the program.*

2

Dare to Be Yourself

It isn't easy to be yourself. Sometimes it gets very lonely. It really hurts when no one seems to understand you. "Am I normal?" "Is something wrong with me?"

Of course you're not normal; at least I hope not. You see, normal means "average." But that's not you. You're different. And proud of it, I hope. Still, it's true that being different and having a mind of your own comes with a price. Average people cannot understand you. "Why can't you be like everybody else?" they ask, annoyed. And then you start to worry. "Yes. Why can't I?"

Now is the time when you are first finding out who you are. That's why you're having such a hard time of it. When you think about it, you are not born with a note attached to your toes listing all your personality traits, your values (what you believe is right and wrong), your interests, and so forth. The job of finding out who you are is left to you and you are supposed to start doing that job exactly now, when you are a teenager. The job never really ends, but you get the major part of the work done during these years of your life.

Some people never find out who they are and as a result they are always apologizing for being themselves, always backing down when they try to stand up for what deep down inside they believe in.

Don't let that happen to you. Make it your business to find out who you are. And just how do you do that? First you have to discover what your personality is—what your likes and dislikes are, your interests, your basic nature. Then you have to think about what your values are—what you really believe is right and wrong. We'll deal with your personality here and talk about your values in chapter 6.

In the search for yourself, the first thing to keep in mind is your uniqueness. You are the only "you." In short, you're a bonafide original who cannot be duplicated. No one can say it, do it, or be it exactly the way you can. If something happened to you now and you left this world, there would be a you-shaped space that no one else could fill. Your "onliness" is symbolized by your fingerprint—distinct from any other person's fingerprints. And scientists have discovered that you have a voice print, too—also distinct for each person. Who knows how many other things about you can be measured and monitored to prove your uniqueness? Science will no doubt find more. But you don't need the latest scientific discoveries to tell you that every single thing about you is different. The combination of your physical and psychological traits make up a completely unusual package.

It's fun being yourself once you know and accept yourself. Here are some suggestions for how to do that.

– FINDING OUT WHO YOU ARE –

Think about yourself for a minute as if you were not *you* but a friend. Make believe you have a friend exactly like you—you in fact. Now—what is this friend like? Is this person intense, lighthearted, fun-loving, generous, sensitive, outgoing, reserved, intellectual, poetic, romantic, witty, wise, playful, devilish—what? By thinking of yourself as someone else, you can sometimes stand at a great enough distance from yourself to see what you are really like. Make a list of ten personality traits that describe you right now, either in your mind or on paper, whichever you prefer.

That list is you. That's your unique "personality print." Or part of it, anyway. Of course you can't figure out your whole personality in two minutes. You may not have been able to think of as many as ten traits. If you did, add another five or ten to your list. If you're having trouble with this list, let me give you some more tips on figuring out what you're really like.

What is your reputation? What do you hear people saying about you? Do they say, "Oh, that Billy, he's the life of the party," or "I always feel so much better after talking to you," or "You're a doer, not a talker," or "Once she promises something, that's it, count it done." When you think about what people say about you to your face, within earshot, and to others, ask yourself—do I agree? Are they reading me correctly? If you agree, if what they say "rings a bell," makes your heart leap just a little bit, add it to the list. But if it doesn't, don't think you have to take their word for it. If people think you're a snob, but you know you're just shy, then you may want to try to change people's perception of you, but that doesn't mean they're right about you.

Don't forget to think about what teachers have said about you to your face and to your parents. "He writes wonderful papers," or "You add a lot of life to the class," and so on. Add in what your parents have said. "You fight hard for what you want," or "You're very loyal to your friends," and so forth.

Another way to find out what you're really like is to ask yourself what you admire in others. This may sound strange at first, but if you think about it, the trait you admire in others is one you usually wish that you had. But I'm here to tell you that you don't have to wish for it, because you have it, only you can't believe it yet. Let me give you an example. I always admired Muhammad Ali. He used to be called "Cassius Clay," but he gave himself a new name. At first people laughed at him, but after a while they accepted it. Then he started telling everyone he was the greatest. Then he made himself the greatest—the world champion heavyweight. I am a lot like him. About seven years ago I made up cards: "Joyce Vedral, star of stage, screen, and radio." I used to tell my classes (I was a high school teacher) "I'm a movie star." Then I would give them the card. They would laugh at me. I laughed too. But now, seven years later, I've been on stage before thousands of people performing in bodybuilding shows and lecturing to large audiences, I've been on television (the screen) and I've done many radio shows. You see. I did what the man I admired did. I "psyched myself up," as the saying goes, and I made it happen. You can make your own "greatest" story by daring to find and be yourself.

Do you admire people who are tough—who don't back down and run no matter how scared they are? If you do, add this quality to your list. Deep down inside you are tough. Time will bring it out. Do you admire people who are outspoken—not afraid to say what's on their minds? Put this on your list. It's only a matter of time before you develop that trait in yourself. Do you look up to someone who is athletic, or someone who has a great sense of humor, or someone who is compassionate and caring? If so, add that trait to your list. You will eventually realize that you, too, possess that trait.

Now you have a foundation—a base. This base is you, your basic personality. The next step is to take a long hard look at that base, that picture that personality print. Study it. Amuse yourself with it. "Hmm . . . so that's me. That's what I'm really like." Enjoy what you see. Be happy about who you are. It's you. Get acquainted with yourself, get comfortable with yourself. Learn to love who you are. We're not talking about faults or negative traits yet. We'll deal with them later. We're talking about basic you.

Now think of this. Suppose someone doesn't like you. That person can't stand the way you're always joking around, or doesn't like "brains," or thinks you're a computer nerd, or thinks it's weird that you write poetry. Too bad. That's his problem. You know who you are. You like yourself. Other people will like your traits and accept them, too. If someone doesn't like your personality, tell him to "travel."

It's the most exciting thing in the world to know who you are and like who you are. Finally you can breathe easy. Finally you don't have to apologize for being yourself. You can say—this is me. If things work out between us, lucky for us. If not, let's go our separate ways and find people who do appreciate us for what we are.

It's no fun when you can't be yourself. It's too much work, and you won't get away with it anyway. Sooner or later the real "self" creeps through.

But what about faults, things you really don't like about your own personality?

– HOW TO DEAL WITH YOUR PERSONALITY FLAWS –

What is a personality flaw? It's something that stands out as upsetting or annoying. In this case, I don't mean annoying to someone else. We've already covered that ground. I mean annoying to you. Suppose, for example, you can't stand the fact that you are shy or timid. The first thing to do is to accept your flaw or "fault" as part of what makes you human. Did you know that Oriental carpets have a small imperfection woven into them on purpose, because perfection, say the weavers, belongs only to God?[1] To be human is to be imperfect.

So. You may be a basically lethargic (slow moving, slow to react) person. You may have a violent temper. You may be stubborn. You may be a little lazy. What can you do? It looks obvious to me. You'll have to work with the material you have and make the best of it.

– MAKING THE BEST OF YOUR HAND –

Norman Vincent Peale, renowned positive thinker and bestselling author, tells this interesting story about the late President Dwight D. Eisenhower. As a boy, Dwight was playing cards with his brothers and his mother. Eisenhower says,

Well, Mother was the dealer and the hand she had dealt me was completely impossible. I began to com-

[1] Lesley Hazleton, *The Right to Feel Bad* (New York: Ballantine Books, 1984), p. 244.

plain that with such a poor hand I had no chance at all. Finally Mother said, "Put down your cards boys. I want to give you some advice. You are playing a friendly game here in your home with your mother and your brothers, all of whom love you. But out in the world, life will deal you plenty of bad hands and those involved may not love you at all. So the lesson is to take whatever hand is dealt you and with God's help just play it out."[2]

Your personality is the "hand" you've been dealt. You didn't pick your parents. They didn't pick their parents either for that matter. You didn't decide which neighborhood you would be brought up in. You had nothing to do with which genes got together to form your personality, and it's not your fault that certain things in your environment have had an influence upon you. But . . . what you *can* do is make the best of your hand. "Play it out." Learn to improve your undesirable personality traits.

– HOW TO BECOME THE PERSON YOU WANT TO BE THROUGH MENTAL POWER –

If, for example, you don't like the fact that you freeze up every time you try to speak to someone of the opposite sex, you can use visualization, or "mental picturing," to change that tendency. Whether you know it or not, you've been reinforcing your undesirable trait by picturing it in action even before you've done anything. Psychologists today agree that there is

[2]Norman Vincent Peale, *The True Joy of Positive Thinking* (New York: Ballantine Books, 1984), p. 252.

a deep tendency to become precisely [...]
ually imagine yourself to be. Such a me[...]
when held long and persistently tends to repro[...]
itself in fact. Visualize yourself as inferior, and the
net result is likely to be inferiority. See yourself as
sick or weak or incompetent, and those characteris-
tics are thereby encouraged to develop. On the other
hand, positive images produce positive results.[3]

You can picture in your mind the positive trait you want
to acquire, and you can actually cause that trait to emerge
in your personality. For example, if you tend to get flus-
tered and nervous when you try to speak to someone of the
opposite sex, stop picturing yourself floundering and being
at a loss for words — stuttering and looking like a fool.
Change the movie. Load the camera of your mind with a
film of yourself being calm and confident. See yourself
laughing and being charming and sophisticated, witty and
suave. See your face smiling and relaxed. See your eyes
sparkling. Imagine the person you are talking to being attracted to you, taking an interest. Every time you start to
dread something and you imagine yourself failing, immediately X out that picture of failure. Cancel it. Replace it
with a success picture.

By practicing this method, you recondition your mind.
It is a kind of self hypnosis. It really works. We'll talk a lot
more about this in chapter 13, "Famous Cop-outs: Breaking the Habit."

Once you have begun a program to improve your weak
or undesirable personality traits, you will feel better about
yourself. You'll get the idea that you're in control. This
feeling, combined with the fact that you now know who
you are, will give you a more positive outlook on life. It

[3]Ibid. p. 277.

...act more positively toward you.
...hor and psychologist, says,

...another rule for mental health that
...ave to take on faith. If you are really,
...f, you will eventually find people who
...nd respect you.[4]

...eling of accepting and liking yourself, faults and all, combined with the sense that other people like and accept you (the real you), will give you what everyone is looking for: a feeling of security.

– FEELING SECURE –

You've probably heard someone say "She just does that because she's so insecure." What is insecurity, and how does it affect one's personality? To be insecure is to lack self-confidence, to be unsure of whether it is okay to be one's self. When someone is insecure he makes every effort to shield himself from being seen—to hide his true self, who he really is—because he believes that this self is inadequate, inferior. The strangest part of the problem is, most people who do this have never taken the time to find out who they really are. They've always been afraid to know. The longer they wait, the more afraid they are. What are they afraid of? They fear that, deep down inside, they are *not* good or worthy. So they hide themselves from themselves, and then try to hide themselves from others.

Insecure people often have trouble in relationships. They can be cold and seemingly indifferent. They find it

[4]Martin Shepherd, M.D., *The Do It Yourself Psychotherapy Book* (New York: Peter H. Wyden, Inc., 1973), p. 41.

difficult to let their friends know how they are feeling. They suppress and hide their true emotions. To friends of such people, this can appear as indifference. It is very frustrating to be in love with an insecure person. You can spend much of your time trying to dig down beneath the protective covering to discover the real person.

Insecure people have a lot of trouble with friends. Very often they will be unable to control jealousy when a friend does well. They see a friend's success as a threat, as if the success of the friend—(whether it be the gaining of a gorgeous new sweetheart, or getting a high mark on a test, or winning a contest)—were a spotlight emphasizing the friend's superiority and their own inferiority. Of course, this kind of thinking is irrational (not reasonable, not correct). The truth is, it's not usually the case that one person's success points up another's failure. Generally, when the spotlight is on, it's on only one person, not two. But insecure people think of everything in terms of themselves and how they look—even when nobody's looking. They are tormented by the idea that everyone will learn the "truth" about them, even when, to any outsider, that truth would certainly not seem very horrifying.

For this reason, some insecure people desperately attempt to hide their feelings of inadequacy and inferiority by pretending to be greater than they really are. They put on airs, act superior to others. They find any opportunity to put people down—to expose other people's faults. Insecure people believe, irrationally, that by lowering another person, they elevate themselves, just as they believe themselves diminished by another's success. The logic is, "If I can show up enough people as phonies and losers, I will look good." Please understand that none of this reasoning takes place on a conscious level. It all happens on a deep, unconscious level. Insecure people are not in control of their reasoning. They are the victims of their own insecurity, and they suffer tremendously. Don't be fooled for a minute by the facade, the "front," or the mask that such a person wears. It is just a cover-up for the shriveled up, fearful, cowering person he is trying to hide.

Once you learn to detect insecurity, instead of becoming angry with insecure people, you'll feel sorry for them, and if you're anything like me, you may even want to help them.

Another problem that insecurity brings is loneliness. Insecure people are afraid to spend too much time alone. They don't really know much about themselves. They don't know what they enjoy. They're afraid to try new hobbies, sports, or intellectual pursuits for fear of looking stupid, first to themselves, and then to an imaginary audience which they picture watching them, mocking them. "You jackass," they imagine this congregation of mockers saying, "you look like a fool doing that."

Secure people, on the other hand, are comfortable spending time alone, so they are never really lonely. They enjoy pursuing their own interests and revel in (rejoice in, celebrate) the prospect of using their time to do whatever they want to do.

– WAYS TO BUILD SECURITY –

As discussed, the first way to build security is to find out who you really are by evaluating your personality, taking into account your strengths and your weaknesses, and making plans to improve your weak areas. But another fantastic way to build permanent, rock solid security is to pursue your interests—to develop your personality. There are many ways to do this. Suppose, for example, you have always been interested in the martial arts. The martial arts can develop not just your physical stamina but your mental tenacity (strength under pressure). If you join a karate class that stresses the Oriental philosophy of inner strength, in time you will develop your own powers of will and mind, and you will begin to think more and more positively about yourself. In short, you will respect yourself.

If you enjoy expressing yourself in words, and if you like reading, you might want to pursue the study of words. If you start underlining every unfamiliar word you come across in your reading then go back and look up the words in the dictionary, write down the meaning, and then re-read the original sentence with that meaning in mind, your vocabulary will increase enormously. More important, your mind will expand because words are the tools for thought. You may, as a result, get all kinds of creative ideas. But most important of all, you will feel good about yourself because you will be developing an interest. In short, you will be shaping and becoming your true self. There's a bonus in this too. You'll score much higher on college entrance exams, and you'll make a fine impression anytime you have to be interviewed because your new vocabulary will eventually find its way into your speech. It's been proven that people with large vocabularies are the most successful.[5]

If you enjoy bodybuilding, you can join a gym or set one up in your basement. Find out how to work out either from an instructor or by reading books (I'll include a couple in the bibliography for you), and follow the program. When you see development, you will feel good inside because you'll know that you did this by yourself. Your feeling of self-worth will rise.

Every time you pursue an interest alone, without the help or company of anyone else, you build your feeling of security. "I don't always need someone with me in order to survive," you realize. "I can be happy alone," you dis-

[5]Dennis Waitley, *The Seeds of Greatness: The Ten Best Kept Secrets of Total Success* (New Jersey: Fleming H. Revell Inc., 1983), p. 95.

cover. "I actually enjoy spending time alone," you say. "In fact I need time alone. I must have it," you conclude.

Think of the relief it is to be able to be happy with or without people. That's a great feeling. And it's one of the best gifts you can give yourself.

There is a final bonus that comes to you when you really know who you are, when you have spent time discovering your personality and your interests. Your parents will eventually step back and realize that you are your own person. They will stop trying to treat you the way they had to when you were a child who needed them to do most of your thinking for you. Parents know that "to have a child is to eventually meet a new person who is not only separate, but different,"[6] but they cannot make that person emerge or come out. It's up to you to do that.

Don't misunderstand me, however. Even though your parents know that you must learn to be yourself, they will probably fight you every step of the way as you show them who you are. Forgive them. It's normal for them to want to continue to protect you, to suffer for you, to think for you. It's hard for them to let go. But even though they fight you, deep down they want and expect you to stand up for your rights and to become your own person. In fact, if you didn't eventually do that they would worry about you. Growing up is hard—on both parents and children. (If you are having extra trouble with your parents, read *My Parents Are Driving Me Crazy*. See bibliography for more information.)

In conclusion, your first step to happiness and true joy is to be yourself. After all, what would people do if they found out who you really are? Would they have to call the police? Would the walls start tumbling down? Would they kill you? Of course not. Instead, they would be delighted to meet the real, one and only you.

[6]Richard Grossman, *Choosing and Changing* (New York: I.P. Dutton & Sons, 1978), p. 102.

The most exciting thing in the world is to find out who you are and then be who you are—and to realize that if anybody doesn't like it, that's their problem. Not yours.

Saying: *Dare to be yourself.*

3

Everyone Is Laughing with Me—Not at Me!

Everyone likes a good laugh, but nobody likes to be the object of the laughter. For this reason, most people spend a good deal of their energy trying *not* to make fools of themselves. People will check their clothing over and over to be sure nothing is wrong. Women will review their makeup. Men will make sure their fly isn't open. People will worry and fret if they have to do something in public such as give a speech, sing or play a solo, or even just go to a party. People are so afraid to make fools of themselves that they will hesitate to ask a question that might indicate they don't know something, for fear of looking stupid. Most people are reluctant to speak to a stranger, even if they want to make friends with that person. They rehearse over and over in their minds what "opening lines" they can use.

While it is normal at any age to have a certain amount

of fear of being laughed at or negatively judged by people, it is certainly uncomfortable, and the more fear you have, the harder it is to act. If you have too much fear, it can even paralyze you. It can ruin your freedom to be yourself and take away the fun of being a teenager. But don't give up hope. Many hugely successful adults who now seem to have no fear whatsoever about what other people think were at one time just the opposite. Lee Iacocca, bestselling author and president of General Motors, a man known for his extraordinary ability to deal with people, reports that as a teenager and a young man, "I was an introvert, a shrinking violet."[1] Norman Vincent Peale says of his teen years, ". . . the most difficult problem I ever faced as a youth was my . . . inferiority complex. I was shy and filled with self doubt. In fact, I lived like a scared rabbit."[2]

You can see that it is quite possible to get over feelings of inferiority. But how? How did a "shrinking violet" and a "scared rabbit" become world famous leaders? They recognized the fact that they didn't like feeling "shrunken" and "scared," and they made up their minds to do something about it. In the same way, you can make up your mind to do something about it, too, and I believe you already have, or you would have put the book down by now.

Let's take physical appearance as an example of an area people are self-conscious about. Most teenagers are not happy with their looks. No matter how good-looking they are, they'll find something to pick on about themselves. An extreme example is seventeen-year-old Jason, who was voted best-looking boy in his high school, but still says,

When I look in the mirror, all I see are my bushy eyebrows. I hate them. Then I see the scars on my

[1]Lee Iacocca (with William Novak), *Iacocca* (New York: Bantam Books, 1984), p. 53.

[2]Norman Vincent Peale, *The True Joy of Positive Thinking* (New York: Ballantine Books, 1984), p. 33.

face. I wonder if people can tell that my teeth are capped. Ever since I had the car accident I keep thinking that my teeth look funny.

Since all Jason sees are his faults, he imagines that they're all everyone else sees, too. But in fact, his schoolmates see everything but his faults, or they wouldn't have voted him best looking in the school. The last thing on their minds are Jason's capped teeth. In fact, the teeth probably make him even better looking. His bushy eyebrows are possibly what makes him so appealing, and his scars are barely noticeable with a magnifying glass.

The next time you catch yourself looking at yourself critically, thinking that the only thing people will see is that zit on your nose or that mole on your cheek, remember that people see all of you, not just your faults. They take in the whole picture.

Another thing to consider is this. Think of someone you like a lot who really gets down on herself. You know, a girl who is always calling herself ugly because she has frizzy hair, or is a little overweight, or maybe has a long nose. You probably don't think that girl is nearly as ugly as she thinks she is. In fact, you probably take into consideration the whole look—and especially the whole personality— of that girl, just as we discussed in the above paragraph (and there's more on personality in the next paragraph.) You probably see the girl's pretty eyes, her beautiful smile, her bubbly manner, the classy way she walks, and so on. In fact, you may say to yourself when analyzing that girl, "Feature for feature she is not that attractive, but when you add up the whole package, she seems beautiful."

– DEALING WITH PHYSICAL
IMPERFECTIONS –

What do you do if there are things about your looks that you just can't stand? You compensate by making people pay attention to another part of you. For example, if you don't like your facial features, get a great hairstyle, and wear clothes that you really like. If you don't like your nose, accentuate your eyes. (Most girls will automatically do this with makeup.) But these are really not the best ways to compensate for not looking perfect. You know the best way to do it? With your personality. That's the part of you that matters more than any physical quality. You must charm people into loving you. Before you know it, they won't really see you at all. Or rather, they'll see the real you, and your dazzling personality will have blinded them to what you don't like about your looks. You will look beautiful to them because your personality or your soul will fill up the shell of your body and face. People whose personalities completely overwhelm any negative perceptions have what is called "charisma"—a magnetic force. When you think about it, you can point to cases you've run into. Isn't there someone you know who is not really very good looking, when you look at the separate parts, but comes across as incredibly attractive? Isn't it true that the person you're thinking of has a great personality?

Those who are charming and full of fun very often find that people say: "You look much better in person than in pictures." No matter how many pictures such a person takes, no matter who the photographer is, it is virtually impossible to get anyone to agree that the picture does that person justice. Why? Because it is impossible to capture the richness of a wonderful personality in a picture. At best, one or two traits might show through.

You can see how personality can go a long way to make

you better looking. And that explains the contradiction between such statements as "Looks aren't important. It's personality that counts," and "Looks are everything." The truth is, both comments are off base, but both reflect part of the truth. In reality, personality affects looks. It creates an aura that surrounds the body. It is, in fact, so important that a person with a beautiful face who does not possess a loving, positive personality will very soon seem cold and empty.

So you see, the truth is, both looks and personality count when it comes to being attractive, but if you had to give up a little of one to get more of the other, I'd suggest you give up the looks and take the personality. With personality you can dazzle them. As the old Brazilian proverb states: He who does not have a dog to hunt with must use a cat.[3]

Make the best of what you do have. If you can't mesmerize them with your gorgeous eyes, magnetize them with your charm. If you can't knock their socks off with your physical charms, blind them with your classy dress style. If you can't take them for a ride with your perfect features, overwhelm them with your outrageous sense of humor.

– WAS MY FACE RED! –

Looks are not the only area of concern to teenagers. One of the most painful things for teenagers to do is to expose themselves to the public eye when performing a task. A good example of this is when each person is asked

[3]Ralph Charell, *How to Get the Upper Hand* (New York: Stein and Day, 1978), p. 80.

to "jump over the horse" in gym class. I'd be willing to bet that every student in that class dreads, at least for a moment, the possibility of stumbling and looking like a clumsy idiot. Here's what happened to Tina, 15.

It was my turn to jump over the horse. I was so nervous that I fell on top of it. When I got up I could feel my face getting red. Everyone was looking at me and some people were laughing. I said "I'm such a clumsy oaf," and ran back to my spot. I could have died.

Poor Tina. She felt obligated to call herself a name. I guess she believed that everyone was thinking that she was a hopeless ox, so she decided to say what she thought they were thinking out loud. Have you ever done this? Have you ever made a mistake and then called yourself a name? Don't do it any more. It isn't a good idea. Every time you say something negative about yourself out loud you give your subconscious mind a message. Your subconscious mind cannot take a joke. It registers what you say about yourself as truth. And your self-image is lowered. What Tina should have done when she stumbled over the horse was to say, "Can't win 'em all." Or she could have said nothing. After all, no one was expecting her to comment on her own performance. She did it out of embarrassment and nervousness.

When you do fumble in front of people, how can you keep yourself from dying of embarrassment? Talk to yourself logically. First, realize that just about everybody in that room is imagining how they would feel if it happened to them. You know that from when you've watched someone else make a mistake. Your immediate reaction was probably "I'm glad it didn't happen to me," and then, if you thought any more about it at all, you probably felt sorry for the person. That doesn't mean you didn't laugh. But think about it. Did you laugh out of meanness? No, you laughed out of nervousness and embarrassment, not because you wanted to make fun of anybody. Or maybe you just laughed because it was funny. Still, you weren't mocking or sneering or being cruel. And neither are the people who are laughing when you make a mistake. Oh, there may be one idiot in the crowd who gets a kick out of seeing others suffer. That person may be mocking you, but you can be sure that the other 99 out of a hundred are on your side. After all, you got it over with. You did the thing they were dreading. You "messed up." Now, if they mess up, it doesn't look so bad for them. You took some pressure off them. In fact, the majority of the crowd likes you more on an unconscious level. You did them a favor by making a human error.

Since you know this, the best thing you can do is laugh at yourself first. That makes you look really together, as though nothing can blow your cool. That way you put people at ease about laughing, and you know they're laughing with you, not at you.

One of the most difficult things to do is to risk being laughed at by exposing the fact that you don't know something. This "exposure" can happen when you ask a question, and it turns out that you really should have known the answer to that question, or, when you give an answer that is completely inappropriate. I'm sure all of us can think back and remember at least one time when we asked a "stupid" question and everyone laughed, and at least one time we gave a "dumb" answer and everyone *roared*!

Most of the time, "stupid" questions or answers are not really stupid. They're just thoughtless or careless. For example, did something like this ever happen in one of your classes? The teacher has just finished giving the homework assignment when someone raises a hand and asks, "Do we have any homework?" We all know that doesn't say anything about whether that person is dumb. People laugh, but if anything, the joke is really on the teacher. Speaking as a teacher, let me tell you that the message is, "People aren't listening to you"—not—"What kind of a jerk would ask such a question?"

Other times someone may ask a question before realizing that the answer is obvious. I took my nephew to a dude ranch. While we were checking in, the brilliant twelve-year-old asked the desk clerk, "Do they have horses here?" To this day I tease him about it.

But what about asking questions that you really want to ask, but are afraid to ask because you're ashamed to admit that you don't understand something? You owe it to yourself to risk the exposure so that you will no longer be ignorant. If you don't ask, you're being stupid, which is much worse than being ignorant. Wise men and women have learned this. Dr. Robert Schuller admits that he nearly failed a class because, when the teacher asked if he had any questions, he was afraid to show "how dumb he was." Schuller says, "That was the biggest mistake I ever made."[4] After that, Schuller reports that he'd rather take the chance of asking and letting people know that he's ignorant than not asking, and thus guaranteeing that he'll remain ignorant.

I must add that after having taught high school English for the past fifteen years, I notice that when a teenager asks a question in class, if the question is funny or in any way different from what is expected, the class will laugh. They are not in any way laughing at the person who asked the question, but rather because they are enjoying themselves. If anything, the class is grateful to the asker for helping to break up the monotony.

[4]Robert Schuller, *The Be Happy Attitudes* (Texas: Word Inc., 1985), p. 25.

– HOW TO OVERCOME
SHYNESS –

Most people who are shy behave that way because they are afraid of how people will react to them. They imagine themselves as the center of attention at all times. They think of a great spotlight focused on them and they believe that people are concerned with every mistake they make in speech, dress, or behavior.

One of the best ways to overcome shyness is to get the focus of attention off yourself by switching the spotlight. You can do this by giving the person you feel shy with a compliment. But make sure your compliment is carefully considered and based upon something you really do admire.

Look closely. Do you like that person's hair, clothing, jewelry, voice, walk, or smile? Then say so. You'll see how quickly you get a positive reaction. Before you know it, you're having a conversation, and the attention is not on you but on the other person—which is exactly what you want, since you're a bit "shy."

Another way to overcome shyness in dealing with people is to get people to talk about themselves. Select a person you'd like to know better. It could be someone who sits next to you in class. You might start by asking "What did you do last weekend?" Before you know it you'll be hearing a whole story. Listen with interest. Laugh at the funny parts. Be expressive. Before you know it this person will be looking for you whenever something exciting happens, hoping to tell you the latest episode in his or her life. Why? Because there is a tremendous shortage of good listeners. You can make a lot of new friends just by listening.

You may be thinking, "But after a while, wouldn't that get boring, just listening to other people talk about themselves?" Yes it would, but you see, it almost never turns out that way. What actually occurs is, the person whom you listen to inevitably starts asking, "So what did you do this weekend?" or "Tell me about your boyfriend." (There are two books listed in the bibliography that can give more details on how to make new friends, *I Dare You* and *Shy.*)

So far we've talked about our unreasonable fears of people laughing at us and people rejecting us. But what do you do when someone really *does* make fun of you or criticizes you in a cruel way?

– DEALING WITH PUT-DOWNS AND HARSH CRITICISM –

When someone criticizes you in a cruel or insulting way, chances are that that person is suffering from feelings of inferiority. Some people like to criticize or make fun of others in order to get the attention and approval of the group. They are always looking for a victim, someone to be the "butt" of the joke. They don't care very much who it is, as long as that person serves the purpose of making them look good. Such people are suffering from feelings of insecurity. They are not sure of who they are, and they don't believe deep down inside that they are "okay." By getting a laugh at someone else's expense, the insecure person thinks he has built a case for himself. He thinks, "I am liked. I am acceptable. I am okay. See—they approve of me. They're laughing at my jokes." Of course this thinking process does not take place on a conscious level. It happens on a subconscious and an emotional-irrational level. The sad part is, such people can never really get enough "evidence" to prove that they are okay, because the opinion that matters the most is their own good opinion, and that they don't have. Once you realize that people who hurt your feelings by making you the punch line of their jokes are really suffering themselves—all the time—you may not be as upset at their making you suffer for just a moment. You can walk away from their problems; they have to live with them 24 hours a day.

Insecure people aren't the only ones who make us feel bad. Perhaps the "criticizer" is insensitive and self-centered. That person may just say what comes into his or her mind without thinking. For example, when you've just gotten a new perm, someone in school might blurt out, "What happened to your hair?" That person isn't thinking about the fact that you've probably been dreading coming to school because you were afraid that everyone would think you look horrible in your new curly hairstyle. That person doesn't stop to imagine how embarrassing it is for you to have your new hairstyle become the focus of attention just when you're sure to be feeling self-conscious about it.

Simply put, some people are not really cruel, they're just incredibly thoughtless. They say what comes to mind without taking time to consider how the other person will feel. They don't really mean harm, but they really do harm.

– TURNING NEGATIVE CRITICISM INTO SOMETHING POSITIVE –

Even if your "criticizer" starts out not caring about your feelings, you can turn the situation around and make that person into an ally. Here are some ways to accomplish that goal.

First, think carefully about what the "critic" or "insulter" said. If what was said is true, agree immediately. For example, if someone just told you that you're fat, and you are, then say: "I know. You're so right. I really should go on a diet." Think of the effect of such an answer. Your insulter will be stopped cold—at first out of surprise, because the usual response to an insult is to go on the counter-attack—"Well, you're not so hot yourself. . . ." or at any rate to become defensive—"No I'm not. You must be crazy." But if you attack, you can be sure you'll get a whole list of other cruel put-downs. You may even end up in a fight. If you defend yourself, your critic will probably add to the criticism, detailing and proving the point. "You're not fat? Look at those thunder thighs. . . ." But by admitting it, you change the whole game. Your attacker will probably feel bad, and may even say something in your defense. "I'm just kidding, you're not that fat, if you lose five pounds you'll look terrific" or "I should talk! I guess I just wanted to get back at you for getting a date with Brian."

You can even turn a negative criticism into something positive by asking the critic to help you. For example, if someone makes fun of your dancing, you can say, "You know, it's true. I really can't dance. I've always admired the way you dance. It seems to come naturally to you. Could you show me a few steps so I won't look like such a jerk." You could take this approach when someone criticizes your hairstyle, your makeup, your dress-style, etc. Remember, do this *only* if you think that the criticism is true—that you really do need improvement in that area. It takes courage and self-control to do this, but if you try it you'll find that you may turn what could have been a painful or tearful experience into a positive one.

Interestingly, when you ask someone for help it tends to make the "helper" like you. Something happens psychologically to the helper, who begins to form a bond with you, to feel in a small way responsible for your progress. That person may even end up defending you against others. For example, if someone who formerly made fun of your dancing is now teaching you to dance and hears someone else being mean to you, he or she may say, "So what?—at least she's trying. She'll get it one of these days." The former "critic" will now be your defender because a part of him—or her—is now invested in you.

Another way to deal with cruel or embarrassing put-downs is to get your critic to see things from your point of view. Wait until things have quieted down, then start up a conversation on "most embarrassing moments." Ask the person what was the most humiliating moment in his or her life. Try to work the conversation around to times when someone criticized and embarrassed that person. Then you can say, "You know, I felt exactly that way the other day when you said . . . to me. I'm sure you didn't mean to embarrass me, but. . . ."

What about parents? They sometimes have a way of criticizing you in a cruel and embarrassing manner. Although it is not their goal to hurt you, very often they do.

– DEALING WITH EMBARRASSING CRITICISM FROM PARENTS –

Did your mother or father ever embarrass you to death by saying something in public like: "If you didn't eat so much chocolate you wouldn't have all those pimples," or "Your zipper is undone," or "Your breath is terrible, don't you brush your teeth any more?" You probably felt like throwing something, or hiding in a crack. Since you can't get violent with your parents (for a million reasons) and you must not seek shelter in the floorboards (the men in the white coats will come to take you away) what *should* you do?

Tell them how you feel. Express your feelings exactly. You can say, "You really embarrassed me when you said that. I felt like crawling through the floorboards," or "When you said that I wanted to start breaking things."

If they don't get the message you might try this. After things cool down, get them into a conversation about the most embarrassing thing their parents ever did to them. This will help them to recall what it feels like to be a teenager. Then you can say, "You know, I felt that way the other day when you . . ." Be sure to control your anger. If you're calm and sweet about it, your parent will be more able to admit his or her mistake.

One of the worst things parents can do to you is to throw something back in your face—something that you confided in them. For example, you may have told your mother that you've been on edge lately because things aren't going well with you and your boyfriend. Later, in front of people, you get a little short-tempered and your mother says, "Just because you're fighting with your boyfriend, you don't have to take it out on everyone else."

Instead of hating your mother for life, make up your mind to tell her this: "When you throw things back in my face that way it makes me never want to tell you anything about me. Maybe I should just keep my life a big secret. I like to talk to you and trust you, but how can I if you . . ."

The last thing your parents want is a communication gap. If you level with them about your feelings, they'll be very careful about throwing things up to you next time. At least give this technique a try. It wouldn't be fair for you to just build up a case against your parents and cut them off without warning. They deserve a chance to change their behavior. Many times they are unaware of how much their behavior hurts you.

We've been talking about feeling inferior, angry, and upset when people put us down or criticize us in a cruel manner. Did you ever notice that on certain days everything seems to bother you more than usual? It could be the weather.

– HOW THE WEATHER AFFECTS OUR MOODS –

Scientists have proven that on cloudy or rainy days the ions in the air change. On gloomy days, there is a tremendous increase of positive ions and these ions act as a depressant to people. On sunny days, there is an increase of negative ions, which act as an energizer or a stimulant to people. In fact, in countries such as Sweden, where the sun shines very little in the winter time, the suicide rate is quite high.

What should we do then, crouch in a corner and be depressed until the sun comes out? Of course not. The saying "forewarned is forearmed" applies here. Now that you are aware that the weather does affect your mood, if you find yourself being a bit irritable or overly sensitive for no good reason, calm down and just blame it on the ions. Then make an extra effort to make yourself happy. Be good to yourself. Listen to your favorite tape, go to a movie you've been dying to see, go to a disco or club with your friends. Make a conscious effort to overcome the effect of the weather on you, and keep in mind that the sun *will* return. Cloudy days don't last forever.

In conclusion, when things don't seem to be going well, instead of assuming it's all your fault, look around. Are your critics down on you for good reason, or do they have problems of their own? Maybe you're just imagining the criticism—we're usually harder on ourselves than the outside world is. Or maybe you're just feeling low because of the weather—too many of the wrong kind of ions. Remember, whether it's bad ions, bad vibes, bad karma, or bad luck, no matter how bad things seem—they will change. And you can help make them change.

Saying: *He who does not have a dog to hunt with must use a cat.*

4

What Happens After You Fail?

Nobody likes to fail. It's depressing. Yet everybody has experienced some form of failure in his or her life. In fact, failure and disappointment are prerequisites to (requirements for) success and satisfaction. Although failure is painful, you can use your feelings of disappointment to spur you on to greater achievement next time, once you've learned how to turn pain and anger into the fuel of accomplishment.

There are three types of failure:

1. When you didn't really try your best and you know it.
2. When you gave it everything you had, yet you still failed.
3. When you really didn't fail, but still you somehow feel like a failure.

This third type of failure involves all kinds of disappointments.

The first failure is easy to handle. It's the least depressing of the three because you know exactly why you failed and what you can do about it. You realize that you didn't give the project your best shot. Whether it's a failed test, a lost game, or a bad decision, if you know you didn't invest the time and energy that you should have, then you can't really be surprised when things don't turn out well. In fact, you would be more surprised if you had done well, given how little effort you put in. It would be like getting something for nothing — almost like stealing, or having the cashier give you too much change on a sale she rings up for you.

So — when you know you didn't put in the effort, failure is easy to accept and easy to correct. The first thing to do is to admit to yourself that you could have, and indeed should have, tried harder. Next, apologize to yourself for taking the easy way out. Then let it go: Don't spend another minute being sorry about what is over and done with. You'll need that energy to fuel your determination to put in more effort next time. You must forgive yourself. After all, you are only human, and to be human is to be lazy and irresponsible sometimes. Finally, promise yourself that you'll give it your best shot next time. Whatever it takes — studying, practicing, or just sheer grit — that's what you'll give it. If that means sacrificing some time on the telephone, in front of the TV or just hanging out, then that's what you'll do.

The second kind of failure is much harder to take — when you feel as if you did try your very best but you failed anyway.

– DEALING WITH FAILURE
WHEN YOU TRIED YOUR
BEST –

What makes you think that just because you try your best you will automatically succeed every time? Where is it written that life comes with a guarantee that "as long as you do your best" you will never fail? If you think that, you've got some truths confused. The real story is, as long as you don't give up when you fail, and continue to do your best, again and again, you will eventually succeed. Success often comes only after many knockdowns—*if* you keep getting up and going back in the ring again. Ari Kiev, psychologist and expert on depression and teenage suicide says,

> The distinguishing mark of the real champions or the Muhammad Alis of the world was their lack of fear of failure. In fact, champions are stimulated by their failures. They learn from them how to go on with the race.[1]

Remember good old Thomas Edison. Well, he was a failure, too. More than a thousand of his experiments failed, but instead of calling himself a loser he took careful notes on what went wrong each time and tried again and again. Eventually he discovered the incandescent light bulb filament which gave us electric lighting as we know it today. Thus a persistent "failure" suddenly became the man who lit up a world previously dependent upon candles and gas. Edison knew all about the hard work that usually precedes "sudden" success. He was the one who coined the

[1]Ari Kiev, M.D., *Riding Through the Downers, Hassles, Snags and Funks* (New York: E.P. Dutton and Co., 1980), p. 19.

expression: "Genius is two percent inspiration and ninety-eight percent perspiration."[2] You may have heard this slogan before. It is often invoked to explain that real success consists of a little talent and a lot of hard and often very frustrating work. "Overnight successes" are often years in the making.

How can you find the strength to try again once you've failed? When you fail at something you feel down on yourself. Whether you realize it or not, you're angry and you're tempted to take that anger out on yourself. But when you do that, the anger just sits inside and eats away at you. You become depressed. Well, there's something else you can do with that anger. You can turn it into energy to help you succeed. You can "sublimate" your anger.

– SUBLIMATION: HOW TO USE ANGER ENERGY TO SUCCEED –

Instead of letting the anger from the failure eat away at you and destroy your confidence, take control of it and direct it against the real enemy—the obstacle in your way. Learn to condition your mind to trigger a "comeback reaction." Here's how it works: You tried to do something—you did your best. You failed. You feel very sad. The thought goes through your mind, "I'm a loser. Nothing I do works." But then you use anger to convert negative energy into positive: "No way am I out for the count. I'm going back in there and slugging it out 'til I win. They'll see—nothing stops me." And with that you get the spurt of energy you need to pull yourself together again. If, for

[2]Ralph Charell, *How to Get the Upper Hand* (New York: Stein & Day, 1978), pp. 161–62.

example, it's a test you messed up on, you organize your battle plan for the next one. You review the questions you failed. You study your notes. You read the books. And, if you need extra help, you ask for it, no matter how much you don't want to look too eager or seem like a nerd, because what you want even more is to beat this thing—to win next time.

And so you get down to business. You work your tail off because you are furious. You can move mountains with anger if you sublimate it and make it work for you instead of against you.

Look what Charles Atlas did. He was the forefather of all world champion bodybuilders—he came before Arnold Schwarzenegger, in fact. But Charles Atlas wasn't always big. In fact, he was so puny that when he went to the beach with his girlfriend, other guys would kick sand in his face and flirt with his girl right in front of him. Charles Atlas got sick and tired of being pushed around. So he joined a gym and took out all that anger on the weights. Every time he thought about someone pushing him around he would pump that iron a little harder. Eventually he got so big no one would dare to approach his girl when he was on the beach with her. But he went further than that—he became a world champion bodybuilder who is still respected to this day. This is a man who knew how to sublimate his anger and convert it into the fuel for success.

You've heard of the late Colonel Saunders. He's the grandfatherly old man who owned all the Kentucky Fried Chicken restaurants. He got mad, too. You see, he was basically a failure in life. He was old and living off social security checks, barely able to pay his food bills. But one day he got mad. Instead of sitting in his rocking chair and feeling sorry for himself, instead of getting depressed and saying, "I guess this is what happens when you get old," he said, "Wait a minute. I'm going to do something to change my situation. There must be a way I could make money." He sublimated his frustration into thinking. He racked his brain. Then one day the bright idea came to him. He remembered the delicious fried chicken his mother taught him to make when she had to go out and work and he was in charge of the other children. He got into his old, beatup car and went around asking restaurant owners to buy chicken made from his special recipe. Finally, he persuaded a restaurant owner in Salt Lake City. Colonel Saunders became a multi-millionaire with Kentucky Fried Chicken restaurants all over the United States.[3] Saunders was old and in a rocking chair and he did it. You're still young—imagine what you could do if you got mad enough.

As a matter of fact, most successful people got that way by sublimating the anger they felt over failure. "Check the lives of the people in *Who's Who in America* and you'll find that those who have succeeded in a major way have been pounded by losing situations. Each . . . has encountered opposition, discouragement, setbacks and personal misfortune."[4]

The best thing about sublimation is that you can use the anger from failure to work for you in any area of your life. For example, you may have just failed in a romantic situation. Someone you really like gave you the "cold shoulder." No matter how hard you tried, this person simply would not come around. You're frustrated. You feel like escaping from the whole situation—going out and getting high or maybe having a few drinks. But instead you take that anger and use it to get something positive done. You put on your shorts and running shoes and run five miles. Now you've not only gotten into better shape, but

[3]Norman Vincent Peale, *The True Joy of Positive Thinking* (New York: Ballantine Books, 1984), pp. 208–9.

[4]David Schwartz, *The Magic of Thinking Big* (New York: Simon & Schuster, 1959), p. 150.

by the time you come home you feel much better about the whole romantic situation. It doesn't seem as drastic. Somehow, on the run, you've worked out your frustration.

Which was more productive, getting high or going for the run? Any frustrating, failing situation can be turned into an accomplishment in another area. You were not invited to the party you wanted to go to. You get mad and start cleaning out a junk closet—throwing out all those things you never use. Then you attack your dresser. Before you know it, you've rearranged your whole room. You've done something you've been wanting to do for a long time but were never in the mood for. You could have used that frustration and anger to kick the dog, rip the phone out of the wall, or start a fight with your mother, but instead you used it to make something better. At least you've got something good to show for your anger. This in itself picks up your mood. The depressing failure situation loses its power over you. You realize that you don't have to be a victim. You feel powerful, you know you can take control of your life and make it go the way you want it to go.

Anger is energy. Electricity is energy, too. Both can be used to harm or to help. You can make electricity work against you (electrocute yourself) or for you (iron your clothing, turn on the lights, etc.). You can harm yourself with anger (get stoned, kill yourself) or you can help yourself (sublimate the anger into another area—accomplish something).

If you have the self-discipline, you can use sublimated anger to get dreaded term papers done, lose weight, or accomplish other tasks you've been putting off. All you have to do is turn your anger outward instead of inward and boom—the job is being done.

No matter how badly you've failed, there's no reason to believe that you are a permanent failure. Not even if that's what other people are saying, too. What do they know? Why should you have to accept their labels for you? Failure is temporary. It's often just a stopover on the way to success. Did you know that a lot of famous people failed miserably in exactly those areas in which they later became huge successes? You want proof?

Woody Allen—Academy Award–winning actor, writer, producer, director flunked motion picture production at NYU and CCNY and failed English at NYU. Leon Uris, author, scholar, and philosopher flunked high school English three times. Liv Ullmann, two-time Academy Award nominee for best actress failed an audition for the State Theater School in Norway. The judges said she had *no* talent. Dr. Albert Einstein, physicist and Nobel peace Laureate, whose theories were the foundations for nuclear energy, flunked his college entrance exams.[5]

Don't let anyone else decide for you whether you are a failure. You decide. Every time you fail at something, just get mad—but not at yourself. Channel the anger. That way, even if you don't end up succeeding in exactly what you originally tried to do, you'll succeed in something else. I know you've probably been told by some well-meaning person, "You can do anything if you put your mind to it." Well, the simple truth is, of course, you can't. Can you fly if you put your mind to it? Can you walk through walls? I couldn't become an opera star, not with my voice. Could your mother become a professional football player? No—but you *can* do a lot more than you ever imagined if you convert your anger to good energy, and give it all you've got.

[5]Dr. Irene Kassorla, *Go For It!* (New York: Dell Publishing Co., 1984), p. 299.

– DEALING WITH JEALOUSY –

One of the worst things you can do is to allow yourself to resent people who do better than you. Fourteen-year-old Trina says,

> I studied all night and I failed the math test, and my friend didn't even study and she got a high mark. That makes me sick.

Why should it? Everyone has different abilities. Trina's friend happens to be gifted in math. But her friend's success has nothing to do with Trina's failure—unless of course Trina lets her resentment interfere with positive action she could take to improve the situation (as in "What's the use, I'll never be as good as X?").

Jealousy is a negative emotion. It's a waste of precious time and energy, energy you could be putting into other areas to improve your life. Catch yourself the next time you begin resenting someone else just because they seem to do well without much effort. Instead, bless them in your mind. Say "More power to you." And you'll find that, indirectly, that power comes back to you, because wishing people well doesn't cost you anything, but it will make you feel much better about yourself.

The third kind of failure involves situations in which you really didn't fail—or not in any very important way— but somehow you feel like a big loser. In such cases, you may be making a mountain of a molehill.

– LET MOLEHILLS BE MOLEHILLS –

Fourteen-year-old Timmy says,

In camp we were playing football and it was the other team's ball. There was a pass and I missed the interception. I got so disgusted with myself I was telling myself I should never play again.

Timmy is disappointed in himself, so he wants to punish himself by not letting himself play the sport he loves. He's being too hard on himself. We all do this. We make one little error and before you know it we're calling ourselves all sorts of names. Haven't you ever done that? You lose your keys and you call yourself an idiot. You forget something you were supposed to bring to school and kick yourself over and over: "Jackass. How could you forget it? It was right on the dresser. You should have put it in your bag last night." And so on.

I say get off your own back. It's bad enough that other people will let you have it when you make a mistake. The least you can do is forgive yourself for making a human error. Instead of calling yourself a jackass, an idiot, a fool, instead of saying, "You should have, you could have, why didn't you," change your inner dialogue. Say: "I blew it this time. Oh well. What's done is done. I'll be more careful next time." And then drop it. That's what you'd tell your mother to do if she kept nagging at you about some mistake you made. So follow your own advice, and stop beating up on yourself. You'll feel better immediately.

Saying: *Turn bad anger into good energy.*

5

I Hate Everybody

Most of us have felt the emotion of "hate," at least for a moment. When you hate, you feel like doing something violent to the person or object you hate. Most often you don't actually do anything. Wisely, you control yourself.

But the emotion of hate, if not dealt with, will turn inwards, against you, where it can do you both physical and mental harm. Doctors today are discovering that many physical illnesses can be traced back to negative thought patterns relating to hate and poisonous hostility.[1]

It doesn't help you one bit if the person you hate really did do something terrible to you and you have good reasons for your feelings. Your hatred won't hurt that person nearly as much as it will hurt you. Then what can you do with the hate you feel toward people?

---

[1]A.G. Manning, D.D., *Helping Yourself with Psycho-Cosmic Power* (New York: Parker Publishing Co., 1968), p. 102.

Basically, there are three groups of people we hate at times: Family, friends, and strangers. Let's talk about family first, specifically parents.

– DEALING WITH FEELINGS OF HATRED TOWARD PARENTS –

"I hate you." "How could you say that to your own mother?" Did such a dialogue ever take place in your house? If so, you probably felt awful afterward. When you feel or express hatred toward your parents, you immediately suffer from guilt. Why? Because with hate comes the fleeting fantasy of violence. You wish your parents harm. In a moment of rage, you might even say or think something like "I wish you were dead." Of course you don't really wish your parents dead. What you wish is that your parents would leave you alone. But the fact that you thought it for even a moment produces a guilt that comes back to haunt you.

In order to deal with your emotion of hate, first realize that you do not actually hate your parents. What you hate is the way they are treating you at the moment. Your hate is magnified by your frustration. Your parents have complete control over your life right now, and that can get very uncomfortable. For example, they can refuse to let you go to a party and you'll end up missing all the fun. They can stop you from hanging out with your best friend. They can get in the way of your love relationship or treat you unfairly by favoring brothers or sisters over you. In fact, the degree of control they have can be infuriating, especially if they exercise that control in a way that seems unfair to you.

However, if you become violent or verbally abusive with your parents, chances are there will be a big blowup and you'll end up feeling worse later. On the other hand, if you merely suppress your feelings, the hate will turn inward, against yourself, and you'll end up feeling depressed. Fourteen-year-old Marge says,

> When my parents won't let me go to a club or a dance, I imagine all my friends having a great time without me, or I think of my boyfriend meeting other girls when he could be with me. I really hate my parents for doing that to me. I just sit in my room all night. I'm so depressed.

What should you do? First, try talking to your parents. Even if you don't end up getting your way, you'll feel much better because you will have expressed your emotions and given them an outlet, instead of letting them fester inside of you like poison. Tell your parents exactly how you feel: "I feel cooped up here while all my friends are out having a good time." Ask your parents if they ever felt that way when they were teenagers. Sometimes by bringing your parents back in time, you get them to realize that you are right. My daughter did that to me recently. I had refused to let her go out on the weekends to the local hangout, an ice-cream parlor. Her immediate reaction was to go to her room and slam the door shut. Of course, that didn't make me sympathetic to her. But she didn't stay there. She came out and talked to me and it worked. She asked me what I did at fourteen. She wanted to know if I had had any friends. I thought about how my life had revolved around going to the place where all my friends hung out, and how I had to nag and beg until my parents let me go. Once I remembered all that, I felt bad about trying to make my daughter into a loner. "She needs friends," I thought. "I want her to be normal. I guess I can't be with her every minute to make sure nothing happens to her. She's capable of taking care of herself to some extent. She will sooner or later, anyway. I'd better let her go." So I told her to go and be home by 10:30.

But what do you do if it *doesn't* work—if your parents still don't understand your frustration? What if your parents seem to be cold and indifferent to your feelings? Get your feelings off your chest by calling a friend. You can cry on the phone and spill out the whole story. If one friend is not home, call another. If no friends are home, call a friendly relative, like an aunt or uncle or maybe a cousin who understands you. Don't worry about imposing on anyone. People really are kind, and they feel for you. Think of yourself. What if a friend or relative or even an acquaintance called you and started crying on the phone and telling you a problem? Wouldn't you listen and try to help? Of course you would—even though you have plenty of troubles of your own. Give people the benefit of the doubt instead of always telling yourself, "They'll probably hang up on me," or "They'll think I'm a jerk."

If talking to someone is not enough, or if there's just no one around to talk to, sublimate your anger by taking a long walk or going to the local Y and swimming or working out. Do something physical. Even dancing would help. You could also listen to calm, peaceful music to relax you.

After you do something physical and have calmed down as much as possible, you might want to get your feelings out on paper. Write a long letter to your parents telling them exactly how you feel. Hold nothing back. Use any language you wish. You'll feel much better once you've gotten it all out of your system. Now of course you will tear up the letter after you read it. Or maybe not. After reading the letter you might realize that your parents should have this. Who knows, it may help them to understand your feelings. Of course, if the language is really bad, you might want to clean it up for the version you give them. But the basic message can be the same. I overheard a father talking about his teenage son. "We're getting along much better these days," he said. "Last week we got into this big argument and later, I found a letter on the table addressed to me. He really got to me. I never knew he was feeling so . . ."

You'd be surprised what you can do if you try. What's the worst thing that can happen? Nothing—things stay the same. But they won't be the same, because at least you'll have gotten that hatred out of your system so that it's not eating you up inside. But the best might happen, too—your parent may understand your point of view and make a change in your favor.

Another way to deal with hatred toward your parents is to try to understand them. They may be doing a lot of things wrong, but they're probably just trying to protect you from what they think will hurt you. Consider their position. Here they are, trying to do what they think is best for you, and there you are hating them for it. They are in a double bind. If they say, "Go ahead, do whatever you want, stay out all night, take drugs, cut school," they'd feel guilty. "You're a terrible parent," their minds would accuse them. They imagine how they would feel if you dropped out of school or did drugs or got killed, and they think, "It will be all your fault because you were too lazy to insist on what was right." (You may be surprised at the word "lazy." But often that's what lenience is—laziness.) If your response to their concern for you is hatred and fury, your parents may think—and even say—"Why did I ever have children? Who knew it was going to be this hard? I can't cope with this." That's why frustrated parents sometimes say things they later regret, like, "I wish I never had you," or even lash out at you with a hand or a weapon in a moment of fury.

By putting yourself in your parents' position for a moment you'll find that your hatred and anger toward them lessens. In fact, you may even feel sorry for them at times.

Even if your parents really are terrible, and you find you can't feel much sympathy for them when you try to see things from their point of view—take courage. People with the worst parents in the world, or no parents, still manage to turn out okay. Psychologists agree that "One seldom sees patients who are not basically healthier mentally than their parents."[2] It seems as if there's a force that operates within every person which works to bring all of us in the direction of sanity. That's why when you look at some people's family history it seems like a miracle that they turned out as well as they did. Dr. Peck tells of such a case:

A thirty-five-year-old, remarkably successful businessman came to see me because of a neurosis [mental problem] that could only be described as mild. He was born illegitimate [out of wedlock] and through infancy and early childhood was raised solely by his mother, who was both deaf and dumb, in the slums of Chicago. When he was five years old the state, believing that no such mother could be competent to raise a child, took him away from her without warning or explanation and placed him in a succession of three foster homes, where he was treated to rather routine indignities [bad treatment] and with a total absence of affection. . . . At sixteen he left his final set of foster parents and began living by himself. Predictably, at the age of seventeen he was jailed for a particularly meaningless assault. He received no psychiatric treatment in jail. Upon his release, after six months of boring confinement, the authorities got him a job as a menial stock-room clerk in a rather ordinary company. No psychiatrist or social worker

[2]Scott M. Peck, M. D., *The Road Less Traveled* (New York: Simon & Schuster, 1978), p. 237.

in the world would have foreseen his future as anything but grim. Within three years, however, he had become the youngest department head in the history of the company. In five years, after marrying another executive, he left the company and eventually succeeded in his own business, becoming a relatively wealthy man. By the time he entered treatment with me he had in addition become a loving and effective father, a self-educated intellectual, a community leader and an accomplished artist. How, when, why, where, did all this come about? .... Together we were able to trace with exactitude, within the usual framework of cause and effect, the determinants [causes] of his mild neurosis and heal him. We were not able in the slightest degree to determine the origins of his unpredictable successes.[3]

If a man with such a background could make it—and he must have experienced plenty of hatred—so can you. Obviously, he got off to a bad start in his teenage years, committing a "meaningless assault," which was probably an expression of all the hatred and anger he felt about his life. But notice that he eventually put his energy into making his life a success. My guess is that when he started to get promotions at work, his self-esteem rose, and he realized he could become what he wanted to be, not what his background told him he would be. I believe it was his will that ultimately saved him. He *decided* not to go under.

Parents are, of course, not our only problems in life. The second group of people we sometimes feel hatred toward is our friends.

[3]Ibid. pp. 236–37.

– DEALING WITH FEELINGS OF HATRED TOWARD FRIENDS –

When you hate a friend it's usually because that friend did something behind your back or because the two of you had a serious disagreement about something which led to a major fight. Now you're filled with rage and hate. What should you do?

First, take time to figure out exactly what happened. Think about what part you may have played in the matter. Was any of it your fault? If you are partly to blame, the best thing to do is to call your friend and admit it. Apologize. Everyone likes to be right. By admitting your wrong, you make it easy for your friend to open up to you and forgive you or even to admit to his or her own share of the blame. Use self-control and don't start bringing up the part that was your friend's fault. That will only start the argument again. Anyway, chances are your friend will feel so warmly toward you after your apology that he or she will immediately say something like, "It was really my fault, I shouldn't have . . ." But if your friend doesn't admit to any wrong, that's okay, too. You are the winner because at least now you're not suffering with all that hate. You have shown yourself to be the bigger person (even if only you are aware of it). This will make you feel so good you won't even care who was in the wrong.

If you are nervous about approaching a friend who is really mad at you, remember, your friend probably feels as bad as you do about the argument, but is afraid to make the first move. Making the first move is a good move regardless of whether you're in the right or not. It's what strong people do.

What do you do if your friend is completely in the wrong? Suppose, for example, your friend went out with your boyfriend behind your back. You feel betrayed. And there's no apology in sight.

First, make it your business to tell your friend exactly how you feel about what happened. If you don't trust yourself to do this in person because you are too angry, write a letter. Instead of name calling and making accusations, talk about how this has made you feel. Say something like, "I am completely furious with you. I thought you were my friend, and I thought you cared about me as a friend, too. How could you do this to me? What happened. . . . ?" If you express yourself honestly and convey how angry and hurt you are by such a betrayal, your former friend may apologize and try to win you back. If not, at least you will have revealed your emotions in a dignified manner and gotten them out in the air. The key is, don't hold them in. Suppressed hatred causes depression.

If your friend does not respond, you must decide what to do. You may feel that his or her good points outweigh the bad, and that you want to be friends again, even if you *were* the wronged one and have to be the one to take the initiative and resume the friendship. Or you may feel that the friendship just isn't worth that much to you. It would probably be a good idea to talk such a tough question out with someone who is more objective, another friend or someone in your family. Just talking it out will make you feel better.

Sometimes the person you're mad at isn't anyone in your family, or one of your friends, or even anyone you know.

– DEALING WITH HATRED
  TOWARD STRANGERS –

You could be driving in your car and get cut off by another driver. You blow your horn in a rage and the other driver gives you "the finger." Now you chase that driver for miles. You both stop. He pulls out a gun and shoots you. Is it worth it? Danny recently had a similarly violent experience, only instead of the driver shooting him, he hospitalized the driver.

I was coming home when I cut this guy off. The guy gets out of the car and starts banging on my window. At first I didn't do anything so he left. Then I thought about it and got really mad. I followed him and when he stopped for a light I opened his door and punched him in the face. His face was covered with blood. The police came. They wanted to arrest me. It wasn't worth it. I just should have let him go.

Seventeen-year-old Danny may have a criminal record —and Danny is lucky. As mentioned before, some people get killed over silly arguments like this.

It could happen on the train or bus, on a movie line, or in a store. You could get into an argument with a stranger and before you know it you're tempted to become physically or verbally abusive. If you do, you go away in a bad mood at best, and at worst, you don't go away at all. How can you deal with the momentary hatred you feel for a stranger?

Think of it this way. Maybe that person had a bad day. He or she doesn't even know you, so there's no way that person could be deliberately trying to insult *you*. The person has problems. Why make his or her problems yours by allowing yourself to be drawn into an unnecessary fight. If someone cuts you off while you're driving, let it go. It's over and done with. Why make a near disaster a sure disaster? So, you "could have" crashed into that person. You didn't. Just be happy you were alert. You were saved the aggravation and injury. The same goes when someone pushes you on the bus. If you make a big deal of it, you could end up in a fight—and maybe in the hospital or a police station. There are too many crazy people in this world to take risks like that. Just chalk the experience up to someone else's problems, and be glad you're not as disturbed as the other guy. Control your temper. It's worth it.

Once you overcome your first flash of anger against a stranger, the momentary hatred you feel just disappears. It was never real so it does not go inward. You don't end up feeling depressed. Actually, you may even feel elated— proud of yourself for using self-control and not getting into a big fight over something stupid.

We can't leave the topic of hate without first talking about revenge. You may be tempted to get even with those who have "done you wrong." You may believe that that's the only way to get rid of the hatred you feel. But you're wrong. The best way to get rid of the hatred you feel is to use the techniques described in this chapter, and then to realize that everyone gets what's coming to him or her in the long run. As Country & Western singer Willie Nelson sings in one of my favorite songs, "There's a whole lot of Karma Goin' Round." Sooner or later what you do comes back to you, maybe not in the same form, but it does come back. When we mistreat others we

produce a karmic or cosmic debt situation which will be collected from us by the law of the Cosmic Universe at some very possibly inconvenient time.[4]

[4]A.G. Manning, D.D., *Helping Yourself with Psycho-Cosmic Power* (New York: Parker Publishing Co., 1968), p. 150.

You may have heard of the biblical saying: "Vengeance is mine sayeth the Lord, I will repay." So let God take care of it, or Karma. You don't have to bother. But if you take it upon yourself to get even, you hurt yourself. In fact, by taking on a job that is not yours—revenge—you produce a karmic debt and something negative will bounce back to you. It's better not to get involved.

This makes sense psychologically as well as karmically. If you do bad things to people you'll subconsciously expect to be punished. You'll actually attract punishment to yourself. We'll discuss this further in chapter 6. For now, take advantage of the idea of karma. Instead of accumulating a "karmic debt," invest good deeds of self-control and dignity in the karmic bank. Then some day what seems like "good luck" will come back to you.

Karma reminds me of the weather. First it rains, then the water goes into the air in the form of vapor, finally clouds form and it rains again. A person's good or bad behavior is like that initial rain. Whatever he rained down on the world will be rained upon him in turn.

Saying: *There's a whole lot of Karma Goin' Round.*

6

What If? Guilt and Fear of Every Kind

When is the last time you felt guilty? Was it the time you hurt your best friend's feelings? Was it when you didn't show up for an important appointment because you were too lazy?

People feel guilty for all sorts of things—and often they should. Guilt, the feeling that one has done something wrong, can be a very helpful emotion. I like to think that guilt was "invented" not to torture and depress us but simply to point us in the right direction—and it can do just that *if* we do not ignore the guilt. You will notice that I am now talking about guilt that comes to you when you have done something wrong. (There's another kind of guilt—unfair guilt—that you have to learn to throw off. We'll talk about that kind of guilt later in the chapter.)

Helpful, legitimate guilt can accomplish its intention only with your cooperation. Instead of ignoring that uncomfortable feeling, the inner voice that whispers "that was wrong," you must stop and think about your behavior. For example, suppose you copied from someone's paper and got a high mark on the test. When you get your mark everyone comments on how great you did—everyone, that is, but your inner voice, which says: "They should only know what a fraud you are. You got the mark by cheating."

When you listen to your inner voice, you build up self-esteem. But there's another voice competing for attention. It's the voice that makes excuses for you. It "rationalizes" (presents false justifications for your behavior) and says: "Everyone else cheats, so what? Anyway, this subject is useless, and the teacher is so boring and unfair. . . ."

If you listen to this voice it can overpower the voice of your guilt. Instead of facing your guilt, looking it straight in the eye, so to speak, and coming to terms with it, you cower and crouch and hide from it. You think that by making excuses for yourself the guilt will disappear, but it doesn't. It buries itself deep in your subconscious mind. Every time you do something that your innermost self knows is wrong and you fail to admit that wrong to yourself and to correct it, you undermine your self-esteem.

Your self-esteem, or what you think of yourself deep down inside, doesn't appear overnight. It is built up gradually over the years, as you grow from childhood into adulthood. Nathaniel Branden, psychologist and author, says: "Self-esteem (or the lack of it) is the reputation a man acquires with himself."[1]

In order to like yourself, then, you have to set a good track record with yourself. You have to build up a good reputation in your own mind by continually daring to face your guilt straight on, admitting to yourself when you have done wrong, and correcting your behavior.

[1]Nathaniel Branden, *The Psychology of Self-Esteem* (New York: Bantam Books, 1969), p. 124.

In order to change bad behavior to good, it helps to know what you really believe *is* wrong. Think of everything that makes you feel bad about yourself, everything that helps to give you a "bad reputation" with yourself. When you do these things, you think about them later and get disgusted and depressed, even when that rationalizing voice starts making excuses for you, trying to tempt you to bury your guilt.

Do you have a long list of such things, things that have subconsciously made you lose faith in yourself? Well, the good news is you can begin today to change all that. You can turn the tables. How? By taking small steps. Pick something from your list and resolve to work on it immediately. Take one of the less difficult things. Maybe something as simple as "not doing homework" (or housework or something similar). Tonight, when you're tempted to skip a homework assignment that would really take only twenty minutes to do, instead of skipping it, do it. See how great you feel about yourself afterward. It's not the homework assignment itself that is so important. It's meeting your obligations. When you do that you have begun to turn the tables. You have made a mark in your own favor on your subconscious mind. Each time you do something to build your self-esteem, your reputation with yourself, it becomes easier to do something right the next time. Your subconscious mind "reminds" you that you are in control, that you can do it, that you are a winner.

Why is it so important to come to terms with guilt—to build up a good reputation with yourself? If you don't, your subconscious mind will eventually force you to pay for your guilt. It will lead you into situations where you punish yourself. Here's how it works.

Psychologists have done studies to prove that criminals set themselves up to be punished because of the unconscious guilt they bear. A criminal will eventually leave a clue to get himself caught; he may even set himself up to be killed by the police or by other criminals. Why? Because subconsciously he believes he deserves punishment. His subconscious mind cannot take the pressure of getting away with things. So he makes sure he gets punished.[2]

But what does this have to do with me, you might wonder. Everything. You see, the same principle of self punishment works for everyone, not just criminals. If you allow yourself to build up a bad subconscious reputation with yourself, even if you do get opportunities to succeed, you will blow them. You will do something to make sure you don't achieve your goal or your dream because subconsciously you won't believe you deserve to succeed. Psychologists have done studies that trace a pattern in the lives of people who, in spite of all kinds of ability, seem continually to have "bad luck," to ruin their own chances for success. Or, having succeeded, they do self-destructive things like going on drugs and attempting or even committing suicide.

No one can cope with a load of suppressed guilt. The only thing for you to do is to deal with it—now. And you are fortunate to be able to begin now, while your self-esteem is just being formed. You may feel as if you're already past that state, but you're not. In fact, now is the perfect, the exact time when you should begin doing the work of facing your guilt and dealing with it—even if it seems to you that there's too much of it and it's too late.

Even older people can do the job, people who have violated their consciences all their lives. People in their thirties and forties and even older can start the job of turning the tables, but it's extremely hard work. They should have started when they were your age—teenagers.

So, if you've been feeling depressed lately, think about whether the cause could be legitimate guilt that you've

[2]Franz G. Alexander, M.D. and Hugo Staub, *The Criminal, The Judge and the Public.* (Glencoe, Illinois: Falcon Wing Press, 1956), p. 139.

been ignoring. Instead of continuing to ignore it and getting more depressed, you could dare to face the guilt head on—and be glad of the opportunity to do so while you're still young and your load of guilt is still comparatively light.

Once you begin to be true to yourself you'll have a different aura about you—you'll radiate positive energy to those around you. You'll tend to look into people's eyes when you're speaking to them instead of keeping your head down. This new attitude will bring opportunities your way because you will look like someone who can be trusted. What's more, you won't be afraid to take on challenges, because in your subconscious mind you'll believe that you deserve success. You'll be expecting it—and you'll get it.

Now that you've come to terms with legitimate guilt, guilt that you should accept and work on, what about unfair guilt—guilt you feel even when you don't deserve it?

– DEALING WITH UNFAIR GUILT –

You may find yourself feeling guilty for things that are not your fault. For example, is it your fault that your parents got divorced? Is it your fault that your father comes home drunk? Are you to blame because your mother sacrificed her career to raise you? The answer is no—and there are *no* exceptions.

When you catch yourself feeling guilty and ashamed of something that is not your fault, before you let that guilt seep in, catch it as you would a rubber ball and throw it back. Don't claim it. It's not yours.

Is it your fault that you're not as intelligent or talented as someone else? Is it your fault that your mother or father is emotionally unstable? Did you pick your parents? Of course not. You didn't even pick your early childhood experiences. What happened to you just "happened." It's no one's fault. Not yours and not anyone else's. What you are now is the "hand" you've been dealt by fate (as in the Dwight D. Eisenhower story). Your job is to make the best of that hand.

Don't fall into the trap of looking for someone to blame for the way you are. Instead, spend your energy working with the material at hand. You may not be perfect, but you're all you have, so work with what you've got.

Another kind of unfair guilt is the guilt you sometimes feel just because you're depressed. You may have heard someone say: "You're a teenager. These are supposed to be the happiest years of your life." Not so. The teen years for many people are the hardest years. Anyway, no particular time is "supposed to be" the happiest. With each person the happiest time is different. Happiness comes when you least expect it.

You will be happy sometime in your life. In fact, you'll be happy many times. Don't worry about when. Just enjoy working on your life right now—doing what you can to make the very best of what you have. And if you're depressed, don't make too big a deal of it. Temporary depression is normal. It's part of being a teenager and questioning your life, wondering what it's all about, figuring out what's right and wrong with your life. It may lead you to make improvements in your life. Besides, chances are you won't stay depressed for long—not if you start trying some of the ideas we've talked about. But if you find yourself in a depression you just can't shake, no matter what you do, and it lasts for many weeks, then you may want to speak to a professional about it. More and more has been learned about how to deal with long term depressions, both psychologically and chemically, and there's no reason to suffer alone when so much help is now available.

Now let's talk about a topic which is often related to guilt: fear. With both deserved and unfair guilt comes fear —fear that something bad will happen to you. For an example of deserved guilt, let's say you've shoplifted something in a store and then you see a salesclerk staring at you. You may fear that you are going to be caught and arrested. Deserved guilt caused this fear. In the case of unfair guilt, you may feel ashamed because your mother is fat, and guilty for being ashamed of your mother. Then, you may start fearing that you too will be fat when you get to be her age. This fear is irrational. It is based upon guilt you put upon yourself for being ashamed of your mother. If you allow yourself to become obsessed with the fear that your parents' destiny controls yours, you may well cause it to happen. This is such a frequent occurrence there's even a name for it: the self-fulfilling prophecy. It occurs when you believe so strongly that something will happen that you make it happen. For instance, if you truly believe that because your mother is fat you too must eventually be fat, you'll begin working hard at making that come true. You'll pick up the same eating habits your mother has and when you start getting fat you may overhear someone in the family say: "She takes after her mother." This will confirm it for you. Instead of rejecting the negative trait, which is within your power to do, you will have claimed it, and your fear will have been the claimer. Be careful. Don't let guilt cause you to claim what need not be yours. You need not punish yourself that way. Make all your self-fulfilling prophecies be *good* ones, not bad ones.

Aside from the fear that comes from both deserved and unfair guilt, there is the fear that comes as a normal result of living—worry.

– DEALING WITH WORRIES AND COMMON FEARS –

Most teenagers worry about what will happen to them when they "grow up." Sometimes adults feed this fear. That's what happened to fifteen-year-old Dina.

Everyone always says what a shame it is to see me grow up because then I'm going to have to see what life really is. I wonder if I'm going to have the same bad experiences just like everyone else. I'm scared that it won't be so easy when I'm independent and my parents are not doing things for me like now.

When people warn you that someday you're going to see what life "really is," they are simply taking the opportunity to dump on you their own bad and maybe angry feelings about the way things are going at the moment. They're probably having a tough time dealing with the challenges of adult life—and that is quite understandable. We all feel that way at times. (And some adults who never really grew up in their minds feel that way all the time. They actually resent responsibilities.) Don't listen to such talk. In fact, when you grow up, and you're on your own, your life will be exciting. Finally you'll be able to decide things for yourself. True, you'll have to get a good job, pay your own bills, and basically take care of yourself, but you'll have complete control of your life. Nothing can be more exciting than that.

It's normal for you to be afraid now, because you're not yet ready to have that complete control. You're still in school, you don't have a steady income, and you probably don't even know for sure what you want to be. You may feel like sixteen-year-old Kathy, who says,

What will happen if I don't get a good education and a good job? I could end up like the bag people who collect soda bottles for a living!

But that's why worry can sometimes be a good thing—it prods you to make sure you do what you need to do to avert catastrophe. Kathy will work harder to make *sure* she gets the education she needs. So—don't get bogged down by worries about what lies ahead. But do listen to the positive part of their message—the part that tells you what you can do now to avoid trouble in the future.

Another worry common to teenagers is that something may happen to their mother or father. Your parents are probably more important to you than anyone or anything else in your life. You depend upon them for financial, emotional, and moral support. So it's quite natural for you to worry every so often about what would happen if they weren't there. But you can't let yourself be tortured by "what ifs." If nothing's wrong right now, why borrow trouble? Tony's father is a cop. He worries that his father may get shot. Jeanie's mother is in the hospital. She worries that her condition may never get better. But right now, thank God, their parents are still here, so the best thing Tony or Jeanie can do now is to enjoy their parents and the life around them. If nothing happens to Tony's father, and Jeanie's mother gets well, a lot of energy will have been wasted on worrying. And if something does happen to Tony's father or Jeanie's mother, worrying about it ahead of time can't prevent it in any case. This is the kind of situation in which worry is pointless. You have to learn to let go of it.

Let's imagine the worst. Suppose something did happen to one of your parents. Worrying can't help but other things can. See chapter eleven for a discussion of this subject.

A very common worry of teenagers is that they will lose their best friend. They fear that their best friend will find someone else to hang out with. The best way to deal with this fear is to say, "What if it happens?" Picture the worst and imagine what you would really do. You would miss that friend a lot. It would be a very painful time for you, but eventually, you would make a new friend. Friends change friends frequently, especially at your age, when your interests change all the time and you often make new friends to go with your new interests. Talk to anyone in school and I'll bet that person can tell you about someone he or she used to hang out with. If you think back, I'll bet you can remember a friend whom you thought you could never get along without. Now you have other friends. Maybe you moved, or the friend moved, or maybe you had a falling out, or maybe you just lost interest in each other —but you did survive.

Chances are you won't lose your friend anyway. If you think your friend is acting "cold," or starting to talk an awful lot to another crowd, this may pass and things may yet return to normal. Don't borrow trouble by blowing things way out of proportion. If you become clingy, you may scare your friend away. Act as though things are fine, and they probably will be. If not, you'll be able to deal with them.

The biggest fear of all—for adults as well as teenagers —is of death. It's scary to think of not being alive any more. It's also frightening to imagine what it might be like if there is an afterlife. Basically, the fear of death is the fear of the unknown. But think of it this way—if you've been trying to do the best you can with your life, what is there to be afraid of? If there is a God waiting to talk to you, great. You'll be ready. In fact, God will probably grab you around and say, "Come on in here. You really tried hard. I saw the way you struggled." Don't let false guilt cause you to imagine a team of devils coming after you to pitch you in the behind with forked implements. And don't spend a lot of time worrying about death even if you've got lots of real guilt. You're still young enough to have plenty of time to mend your ways.

Finally, there are all sorts of little fears that plague us. Some of us are afraid of the dark, others fear speaking in public, and others fear trying something new. I say the best thing you can do is face your fear head on. Plunge in. Do the thing you fear and you'll defeat that fear.

Fourteen-year-old Rita was afraid to walk into her karate class the first day because she was the only girl in the class. But she walked in and got into the lineup. Now, a year and a half later, she's talking about going all the way to black belt, and what's more, she says, "I'm glad there are not a lot of girls in the class. There's no one to fool around with. I had to get serious and really learn how to fight."

Fifteen-year-old Christine was afraid to walk out onto the stage in Carnegie Hall to play before thousands of people in a piano playing contest. But she forged ahead and pushed herself out there. She took her seat at the piano and won first prize.

Seventeen-year-old Tommy was afraid to enter the marathon. But he entered anyway and even though he only placed somewhere in the middle, you could hear him bragging, "You should have seen me. I kept going even though I was dying, and I finished."

Are you afraid to go in and apply for a job? Walk in, open your mouth, and say: "I'm here to apply for..." or "Do you have a job application for..." If you don't get the job, you'll still feel good about yourself for having had the courage to apply.

Do the thing you fear. Beat the fear.

In conclusion, walking around with a load of guilt is like having a fifty-pound potato sack on your back. It gets horribly heavy after a while and makes it difficult for you to function. Carrying a load of fear is like trying to move with ropes tied around your body. Guilt weighs you down, fear ties you up, and paralyzes you. Shuck off the load of guilt. Snap the cords of fear. No wonder you've been feeling down. Be free and walk in the sunshine. Enjoy every minute of your beautiful, unique, exciting life.

Saying: *Don't claim it.*

7

Nobody Loves Me

Does anybody love you? When someone loves you, that person is patient and kind, loyal at all costs, always believes in you and expects the best from you—and would never budge an inch when it came to defending you.

That person would never be envious or jealous of you and never be rude, touchy, or irritable with you. He or she would never hold a grudge against you no matter what you did, and would never pick on any of your faults.

We're all in the same boat. I doubt that anyone reading this book can honestly point to one person who really loves him or her according to the above description. Why? Because nobody is perfect, and what is described above is taken from the biblical definition of perfect love.[1] But I'll bet you can find people who fit parts of that definition. For instance, is there someone in your life who is always kind

[1] I Corinthians 13:4–7.

toward you? Is there someone else in your life who is loyal to you at all costs? Think hard. Is there someone who always believes in you and expects the best of you? Is there a person who would defend you to the death—who would never budge an inch? Is there someone who is never envious or jealous of you? Is there another person who is never rude, touchy, or irritable toward you?

Most likely you've thought of a few people. Probably there was some overlapping. You may have surprised yourself when you realized who really loves you. I'll bet your mother's name came up more than once. Probably you have a friend or two whose names come to mind. More than likely an aunt or uncle got in there somewhere, and your grandparents probably showed up, too. If your boyfriend or girlfriend's name didn't come up, I think you should ask yourself why you're going out with that person.

So, it looks as if, although nobody loves you perfectly, completely, a number of people do love you in the best way that they can.

Why then do you feel unloved? Because when you grow from child to teenager, you must give up your child's fantasy of perfect, loving parents who can and will always fulfill all your needs. This is a part of growing up, and it's one of the hardest parts. It means accepting your parents as imperfect and human, as we all are. It means looking beyond them to meet some of your needs, as we all must do. And it means becoming self-sufficient, able to look within yourself for some of the approval and acceptance we all need.

But let's think about this last statement for a moment. Haven't you already decided that you are a basically worthy person, someone whom you approve and respect? And haven't you committed yourself to continuing to build a fine reputation with yourself (self-esteem)? As long as you love (accept, approve of, respect,) yourself, you will be able to go out there and find some people who *will* love you. And you will be able to deal with the fact that other people *won't* love you. It will not be a police emergency that everyone you meet immediately accept you, approve of you, etc. In other words, you'll be able to cope with rejection.

– COPING WITH REJECTION –

Rejection is painful. If someone does not accept your personality, however, think of it this way. Maybe that person cannot appreciate your unique qualities. Perhaps you are unusual, creative—you stand out above the crowd. Maybe you're too much for some people to handle. Did you know that most creative geniuses had to go it alone? They were "rejects." Nobody understood them. But now everyone looks up to them.

Even if you don't consider yourself to be a creative genius, you certainly are different, not like anybody else. Maybe you would be better off without such people (the ones who reject you) in your life. For example, here's what happened to Roxanne. Sandy and Denise rejected her as a friend. The three girls were friends for two months, but Roxanne was always hanging back—being a "spoilsport." She refused to sneak out the window with the other girls in order to stay out all night when they slept over at her house. She often took the victim's side when Sandy and Denise would put somebody else down and hurt that person's feelings. One day Sandy and Denise picked an argument with Roxanne and ended up saying, "We can't stand your guts. You're a stupid baby. Half the time you act like an old lady." If Roxanne had had low self-esteem she would have said to herself, "What's wrong with me? Nobody likes me. I don't know how to act. I should be more daring. I shouldn't be so softhearted." But instead, although Roxanne felt bad, she realized that she was better off without these friends.

A few weeks later, Roxanne started hanging out with a new crowd, people more like herself. Now she's much happier. What seemed at first like a bad thing turned out to be good.

Are you a "loudmouth" always making jokes? Perhaps you overheard somebody say about you, "I can't stand listening to all that wisecracking." So what. Don't feel bad. Other people will love being around you. They'll appreciate your lively sense of humor. They will become addicted to your energy and will depend upon it to pick them up and get them going when things are looking dull. And they are the kind of people whom you'll enjoy.

Are you too quiet? Do people overlook you at big parties and ignore you even in small groups? You'll find other people who love to have the floor, who will be happy to have a quiet friend. They may prefer to see you one on one, instead of in groups, especially if they want to confide in you.

Do people think it's weird that you're a birdwatcher or ballet dancer or black belt in karate? Well, isn't that their problem? No matter what your personality is like, there are people out there who will be crazy about you. Just keep meeting new people until you find a good fit.

Seventeen-year-old Dom lost most of his friends. It happened when he became "religious." Dom used to be wild. He would steal, do drugs, vandalize the school, smash up his father's car—the works. Then he got what he calls "saved." He started talking to his friends about God all the time. "He's no fun any more," they said. "We get nervous being around him. He won't even drink any more." So they stopped hanging out with him.

But was Dom really being rejected? He says,

At first I felt really bad—like a reject. But then I realized that I really have nothing in common with them any more. Without even trying, I met a whole bunch of new friends in the young people's group at church. I still have one or two friends from before, but we're not that close.

Whether you're a holy roller, a bookworm, a jock, or a prima ballerina, you'll find someone who thinks you're terrific, someone who would love to be around you.

Dealing with rejection from friends is one thing, but what do you do when your own parent seems to reject you?

– COPING WITH REJECTION FROM A PARENT –

Parents refuse to give you love, refuse to accept your personality, for a variety of reasons.

Your parent and you may be experiencing a personality conflict. You may remind your parent too much of his or her self. When your parent picks on you, it may be because of an inner conflict he or she is experiencing without even being aware of it, or a desire to shield you from some of the pain he or she has suffered as a result of that personality trait. For example, if your father is a very stubborn man, he may accuse you of being pigheaded; he may continually criticize you for that trait. If your mother is overly sensitive, she may insult you for being a "crybaby." In both cases, they're probably just trying to get you to avoid their problems.

Personality conflict can involve other problems, too. It is possible that your parent resents the fact that you are not an "easy child." You question everything, you always have an answer. You're not docile. You stand up for your rights in no uncertain terms. This makes you "difficult."

Very often in such a situation your parent falls into the trap of asking you why you can't be like a brother or sister who is much easier to handle. Your parent doesn't realize that by asking you to be like someone other than yourself, he or she makes you feel that you are not liked for who you are, and that you interpret his or her words to mean, "I reject you."

No parent starts out by saying to him- or herself, "I don't like my child. I don't accept him (her)." As you grow up, things happen between you and your parents that really aren't anybody's fault. It's just the way the chips of life fall.

True, your parent should be more understanding, and perhaps could benefit from reading psychology books or going to a psychologist to try to find out the basis for the problems between you. But unfortunately, your parents are not perfect. They are human, too. They may not be willing to go through the initial agony of exposing themselves to the introspection (the process of looking into one's self) that psychotherapy or self-analysis would require. In addition, your parents may not even believe that anything is wrong. They may be preoccupied with the business of surviving—earning a living, taking care of the physical needs of the family, and dealing with other family or personal problems.

Sometimes a parent's rejection of you may go very deep, so deep that it reaches into your parent's own past. Maybe your parent was rejected by his or her parent. Dave's father was put into a home when he was seven years old. His mother never came to visit him once. When Dave got out he found his mother and discovered that she was living happily with a man she had met shortly after she put him away. When he asked why she never came to visit him, she told him she was too busy. Dave's father eventually became successful, married, and had Dave and two other children, of whom Dave was the firstborn. Unbeknownst to Dave, his father never really wanted to have children, but Dave's mother insisted. When Dave was born his father felt frightened and threatened. On some deep, subconscious level, Dave's father "remembered" all of the negative things that had happened to him as a child. As Dave grew up, his father was extremely critical of him. It seemed as if Dave could do nothing right.

It is clear that Dave's father's rejection of Dave has something to do with his own rejection by his mother. It would probably take a good deal of therapy to get to the root of the matter. The problem is, Dave's father is too terrified to face the situation. He will not go to therapy. So what can Dave do? He has somehow to find the inner strength to cope with the fact that although his father seems to be rejecting him, what he is really doing is playing out some scenario from his past—a replay of a terrible tragedy that happened to him when he was a child. Although Dave suffers as a result, his father's behavior has nothing to do with Dave.

It is not your job to become a therapist to your parent. But if your parent behaves toward you in a seemingly irrational way, it would pay you to take the time to try to analyze what is going on beneath the surface. Remember, if your parent is really rejecting you, then he or she is deeply disturbed about something that is not your fault at all. Your parent is in a lot of torment due to problems that he or she cannot face. Your parent has probably spent an entire lifetime trying to run away from whatever it is that is making him or her reject you. Being on the run from one's own self is not fun.

Sometimes parents aren't really rejecting their children, but are very insensitive about what they say. This happens frequently between parents and children whose personalities are extremely different. Many parents never stop to realize that just because you are their child, that's no reason to believe that you should be anything like them. For instance, a friend of mine has a daughter who is very fastidious. She takes two hours to get ready in the morning. My friend, on the other hand, gets dressed and out of the house in less than half that time. My friend would tell me of the constant battles she would have with her daughter. She would say things, like, "What's wrong with you? You're not going to a grand ball. You're so slow. Get a move on. No one else I know takes that long to put on their makeup. Who do you think you are?" But then my friend took a three week trip with her daughter, traveling all around Europe. By the time she came back my friend reported:

> I'm almost ashamed to say this. I never really knew my daughter until now. At first I would get annoyed with her constantly. Why couldn't she hurry up, why didn't she want to rough it like me? Why couldn't we walk instead of taking a taxi? It's only a half-hour walk. But then I started to get glimpses of her. She's such a lady, I thought. She really has a lot of class—and she knows exactly how to put an outfit together. I also noticed how gentle and charming she was in dealing with people. "She must wonder about me," I thought. I throw on anything and go out there like a steamroller. Yet she never criticizes me—and I'm always on her back. I realized that day, with a little embarrassment, that all the time I have lived with my fifteen-year-old daughter, I never really knew her until now, and I also felt sorry for the many times I needlessly picked on her just for being herself.

My friend learned that her daughter has a personality of her own and that it's perfectly fine for her daughter to be different from her. Not all parents come to such realizations by themselves. But sometimes you can get them a little help in coming around.

If your mother and father seem to be rejecting you because you're so different from them, instead of allowing yourself to become furious and then depressed, have a kind, calm talk with them. Fourteen-year-old June tried it.

My mother kept picking on me because I didn't want to keep up my piano lessons. She's a great pianist and I know she was really expecting me to follow in her footsteps. Whenever I would find an excuse to miss piano lessons she would say things like, "You're so lazy. I can't believe you're my daughter. Where did you get your genes," etc. Then one day I sat down on the couch with her and hugged her and said, "Mommy, I love you. I really admire some of your traits. You're such a unique person. But I'm not like you Mom. It's hard to be like you. There's only one you in the world. Don't worry. I do have some of your strong traits but I just don't have them all. I'm not as interested in piano as you are and I don't get as involved as you do in things." My mother laughed and she seemed happy. Then she said, "You know you're right. You do have *some* of my traits." After that she didn't nag me as much. She seemed to have a different attitude.

If you let your parents know that you are not rejecting them by not being like them (June did it by telling her mother that she admires some of her traits), and that you think that in their own way they are special and wonderful, your parents will suddenly step back and do a double take. Instead of having tunnel vision, looking at you only with an eye to molding you into what they want you to be, your parents will feel less threatened by the fact that you are different from them. If you don't make them feel rejected, they're more likely to accept you. Seems like simple human nature, right? When you come to think of it, how often do parents really get to hear from their children they are special? By having such a conversation with your parents you'd be accomplishing two things at one time. You'd be helping them to accept you for what you are, and you'd be helping them to see themselves as special—both of which would make them very happy.

What can you do if your parent, no matter what you do, still does not seem to like you? Sometimes not much—except be happy if you have one parent whom you can relate to, one parent who seems to love and understand you. But what if neither parent seems to love you—if you feel totally rejected by both parents?

– DEALING WITH REJECTION FROM BOTH PARENTS –

All is not lost. If you cannot have a two minute conversation with either parent without getting into a major battle, you can always find another adult who understands and accepts you. You may be surprised to learn that a parent "substitute" is almost as good as a real parent. Of course, your real parents are still your real parents, and they are providing food and shelter for you, but somehow they cannot provide for your psychological needs. In order to survive, you must provide for those needs yourself by finding a "surrogate" or substitute parent. Where can you find one?

– FINDING A SURROGATE PARENT –

Surrogate parents are all around you. You can develop a friendship with an aunt or uncle. You can get close to one of your friend's parents. Maybe one of your grandparents can fill the need.

Sometimes the most unlikely people end up being good substitute parents. Your basketball or swimming coach may be the one. It can be the owner of the local ice-cream parlor or pizza shop, the gas station owner, the family doctor, a friend of one of your parents, a teacher, or even the school custodian.

Any adult with whom you feel comfortable and with whom you can talk freely is perfect for the job. But how do you get this person to "serve?" Of course, you don't go up to someone and say, "Excuse me. I'm being rejected by my own parents and I'm looking for a substitute parent. Will you be the one?" What you do is let it happen naturally. Think of an adult you already know, someone whom you look up to or like a lot. You've probably already developed something of a relationship with that adult. All you have to do is build on it. Get into a conversation with that person about how he or she felt as a teenager. Ask whether his or her parents were accepting or rejecting. Work the conversation around to trouble that person may have had with parents as a teen. Before you know it, that adult will probably ask you how you're getting along with your parents. You can tell that person all about it.

But that's not the only thing your substitute parent can do. That person can serve as an adult friend—a wise person who loves you and believes in you, who expects the best from you and who is happy whenever you succeed. You'll be surprised when you see how much better you feel once you develop such a friendship with an adult.

Psychologists who have studied cases of teenagers who seem to make it in spite of rejecting parents usually come up with an adult somewhere in that teen's life who believes in him or her. Usually it was the teenager who, perhaps without realizing it, sought out the adult and initiated the friendship. Nothing is stopping you from doing the same.

By the way, don't worry that the adult will not want to be bothered. Most adults are flattered and surprised that a teenager is interested in talking to them at all. They will be delighted to serve as confidants. It will make them feel important and needed. They will get as much out of the relationship as you will. But you have to take the first step. You have to make an investment in your future—in your psychological well-being.

Finding a surrogate parent is not the only thing you can do to fill the empty space in your life. You can get genuine love from others, too, by taking the first step—by reaching out and helping someone who is less fortunate than you are.

– GETTING LOVE BY GIVING LOVE FIRST –

It's a surefire formula. If you give love to someone, not expecting anything in return, that person will love you back. It happens just the way an action produces a reaction. If you punch someone in the head, you create anger. You can be sure of that. Am I right? Well, you can be just as sure that if you do something loving and kind for someone, that person will radiate a positive, accepting, loving feeling toward you. Alfred Adler, a psychologist who cured many depressed people, used to tell suicidal patients who were suffering from lack of love to go out and do something to please one person each day for two weeks in a row. Without fail, when the patient followed Adler's strange prescription, that patient was cured.[2] Why? By getting involved in someone else's troubles the patients forgot their own troubles. They realized that they were not the only ones to feel alone and rejected, and this knowledge somehow comforted them. No one likes to feel as if he or she is the only one in the world who is miserable.

But I suspect that the most important reason for the cure is the honest warmth and love that comes back to the person who does a kind deed. The person suddenly feels wanted and needed. Think of a time when you did something loving or generous for someone—something that came from your heart. Sixteen-year-old Tanya says,

> I worked as a camp counselor with the little kids (six-year-olds). My job was to teach them how to ride the two-wheelers. I can't explain it, but I felt really good that summer—like a warm feeling. All those kids really loved me. I'll never forget it.

You are needed. There are thousands of people out there who would love you if you would just take the first step. You could help someone to learn to read, you could volunteer to work with the elderly in your community. There are always volunteer jobs for teenagers at the local hospital. Think of all the lonely, neglected people who are sick and helpless. You could cheer them up. And who knows, you might meet your future husband or wife in such an activity. It's a strange thing about life. When you forget all about yourself and start doing something to help someone else—"Boom." Good things of all kinds start to happen to you, too.

For practice, why don't you start doing some loving acts

[2]Alfred Adler, *What Life Should Mean to You* (New York: G.P. Putnam's Sons, Perigree Books, 1931), pp. 158–59.

right in your own home? Volunteer to help your younger brother or sister with homework. Offer to do your older brother or sister a favor. Clean up the house for your mother while she's at work. Take down the garbage without being asked. Buy your father a surprise and watch his face light up.

I was going to tell you that you don't have the power to snap your fingers and make somebody love you. But I changed my mind. Well, you can't really do it by snapping your fingers, but it's almost that easy. If you express love for someone else through an act of kindness, that person will not be able to help loving you back. It's a sure thing.

Now that you know that, there's no reason for you ever to feel unloved. You need never again have the feeling that "nobody loves me."

What else can you do to make yourself feel loved? Treat yourself well. Love yourself. Instead of being cruel to yourself, be kind. Think of what you really enjoy doing and do it. Take a long, hot bath. Put on your favorite music. Eat your favorite food.

In conclusion, do whatever you have to do to fill your life with love. And remember, everyone in the world experiences rejection from time to time. No matter how hard you try, you simply "can't win 'em all," but you sure can win some of them, so if you get rejected by one person, remember there are plenty of other people out there who would love you if you gave them the chance.

Saying: *You can't win 'em all, but you can win some.*

8

Yes You Can

"I can't." "It doesn't pay." "Who cares?" "Nothing matters." "It's impossible."

What is negative thinking? It's the belief that there's no use in trying because nothing can be done. It's the mind's easy way out! If you believe that nothing can be done, then the pressure to act is off. You don't have to do anything.

Well, you can, it does pay, you do care, it does matter, it is possible. Believe it. It's true.

Momentary pessimism is normal. It's a way of getting a second wind when something bad has happened to you. For example, you have just found out that your best friend has been seeing your boyfriend/girlfriend behind your back. You are furious and you say, "You can't trust anyone in this world. Everyone is out for themselves. What's the use of having friends?" But after you calm down, you must get up and try again. Give life—and friends in general, if not this particular friend—a second, a third, a fourth—an endless number of chances. It'll pay off in the long run. And if you don't, you will close yourself off to the future.

Bad experiences happen to everyone. If you let a bad experience determine what you expect for the future, you'll get what you expect—more bad experiences. You will actually attract them to yourself. You set the "law of attraction" into motion. Your negative expectation behaves exactly like a magnet.

On the up side, the same way you draw negative experiences to yourself by expecting them, you can attract positive experiences by thinking positive.

Did you know that you can change your whole life just by changing your thinking? This is your opportunity to turn your life around. All you have to do is reverse your thinking.

When you're thinking negative, life is tough. Even breathing seems like work. You have trouble getting out of bed in the morning. But if you believe that this is going to be your lucky day, you leap out of bed, ready to go.

Your goal is to develop the habit of positive thinking.

– WHAT IS POSITIVE THINKING –

Positive thinking is expecting the best without proof ahead of time. It's exactly the same thing as faith. "To have faith is to be sure of the things we hope for, to be certain of the things we cannot see."[1]

If you play on a team, your teammates have faith that

[1]Hebrews 11:1.

they can win the game. Think of the effect of someone saying, "We're going to lose today. We have no chance against them." All the team members would gang up on such a person and tell him to shut up and stop being so negative. The team would realize instinctively that negative thinking could hinder their playing. In fact, think about what coaches do. They psyche you up, because they know, both from instinct and from studies that have been done on the subject, how crucial positive thinking—being "psyched"—is to winning the game.

If you want to improve your life, you have to make a conscious effort to change your thinking from negative to positive. Positive thinking can do more than help you to succeed in small daily tasks; it can help you to do the seemingly impossible. Look at what can happen when you don't stop to ask yourself if you can:

A woman and her son had to stop to change a flat tire. While her son was changing the tire, the jack slipped and the truck fell on him. It weighed seven hundred pounds. Without even stopping to think, the woman lifted the truck and held it up until her son could crawl out from under it.[2] What gave her the sudden strength to perform such an impossible feat? She didn't stop to ask herself if she could. She didn't waste energy doubting. She just did it.

With faith you can do the impossible. You can move mountains—and trucks.

> If ye have faith, and doubt not . . . ye shall say unto this mountain, be thou removed, and be thou cast into the sea; and it shall be done.[3]

[2]Dr. Wayne Dyer, *Pulling Your Own Strings* (New York: Avon Books, 1977), p. 12.

[3]Matthew 21:21.

– HOW TO MOVE *YOUR* MOUNTAIN –

If you have a positive mental attitude you can move the impossible mountains in your own life. You can overcome any obstacle in your way. What is your "mountain"? What is making you miserable right now? Is it a course in school that you can't pass? Is it your inability to get a job after school? Is it your loneliness—your lack of a boyfriend or girlfriend? Is it a drug or alcohol problem? Say to this mountain: "Be thou removed." Order the obstacle to go away.

By making the statement "Be thou removed," you psyche yourself into believing that you can overcome the problem. And once it's psyched, the mind finds a way to make your wishes become reality. Suddenly you think of solutions to your problem.

But what if you just don't feel very positive? What if everything is going wrong, and when you get up in the morning, you begin to think of all the bad things that might happen to you that day? Try this. The first thing you say when you get out of bed is: "I believe. I believe. I believe." You must say it out loud and say it three times.

Once I was forced to stay in a seedy hotel in Paris because my plane had been diverted because of a snowstorm. I had missed two flights and my baggage was sent somewhere else. I was reading Norman Vincent Peale's *The Power of Positive Thinking*. That's when I read the paragraph suggesting the "I believes."[4] I went to bed. In the morning I started thinking about the dreadful day ahead of me: "I'll probably miss my flight again," "I'll bet my bags

---

[4]Norman Vincent Peale, *The Power of Positive Thinking* (New York: Ballantine Books, 1965), p. 127.

are lost," "These people don't know what they're doing." Suddenly I remembered what I had read the night before, and without really thinking I caught myself saying out loud: "I believe, I believe, I believe." Then I started laughing at myself. I sounded kind of stupid. But somehow my mood immediately changed. I was happy.

When I arrived at the airport there was trouble. But I was now in a good mood and didn't panic. I went from one counter to the other until things were straightened out. I got my flight. When I arrived, my bags were not there, but I was told they would arrive that night and be delivered to my hotel. I gave the airline the address and left. After a relaxing evening the bags did arrive. Everything was fine. I can't prove that the "I believes" caused me to catch my flight and find my bags. But I'm quite sure that they put me into the kind of relaxed, positive mood that encouraged good things to happen. After all, if I'd been thinking the worst, chances are I would have been irritable and nasty with the airline personnel, and they wouldn't have been as cooperative. I could have attracted "bad luck" to myself by my negative thoughts. Just saying those two words three times changed everything. Try it. It may seem foolish, but it's fun and it works. Say it now as you think of your "mountain," your huge, overwhelming problem. "I believe, I believe, I believe."

There are other ways to help yourself to think positively. Remember the three cards I told you to write up, the ones with your goal in a word picture? (see p. 10) These cards are a positive reminder to you that the goal which now seems so impossible will eventually be realized. Also, do you recall the success movies I've asked you to play — movies canceling out the failure movies, movies in which you see yourself behaving exactly the way you want to behave, doing exactly what you want to do? These movies will help you to expect good things to happen to you, and that expectations will cause them to be more likely to happen.

Everyone knows about hypnotism. A person who is hypnotized can do things he or she can not ordinarily do. How does the hypnotist get the subject to do what was previously "impossible?" The hypnotist puts the subject into a state of total relaxation and then tells the person that he or she can and will do that "impossible" feat. The subject believes this because the subject's conscious mind is asleep. Only the subconscious mind is listening, and the subconscious mind is always cooperative. It is a willing servant. It will do as it is told.

You can be your own hypnotist. By using the above methods you are giving your subconscious mind messages: "Achieve your goal." "Attract good luck." "Have a good day." "Overcome the problem." "Be happy." "Meet the right person." Sooner or later you must succeed. The mind is the most powerful aspect of the human being. A positive mind will produce a positive life. It's as sure as the law of gravity.

In order to give yourself the best possible advantage in conditioning your mind to think positive, it's important that you pay close attention to what you say.

– NEGATIVE VERBALIZATIONS –

Beware of negative verbalizations. We talked about this before in connection with putting yourself down. Don't do it. And don't put additional stumbling blocks in your own way but saying things like, "I'll never be able to do that," or "I'll never learn this subject," or "This will never work."

I was recently teaching a very heavy woman how to work out in order to get in shape. We were doing abdominal work, and the woman, who had never done a sit-up in her life, attempted to lift her huge body off the sit-up board. She quickly flopped down, after raising herself about two inches. "I'll never do this," she said. "I can't." I immediately said, "Don't say that. Say 'I will do this. I can do it.'" "I was just kidding," she said. "Your subconscious mind can't take a joke," I replied. Then she laughed, and to humor me she said: "I can do this. I can do this." And with that she proceeded to do four full sit-ups!

What was it that made the woman suddenly do what she "couldn't" do? She removed the obstacle she had placed in her own way—her negative words.

Stop stepping on your own feet. Get out of your own way by removing from your spoken vocabulary all expressions that express inability to do something.

Think of the last time you said, "I can't," "there's no way," "it's impossible," or the like. Write it down here, only replace the negative words with positive words. For example, if you said, "I'll never be able to finish this term paper," I say, "I will be able to finish this term paper." Make a list of all the things you "can" and "will" do.

1. I can . . .
2. I will . . .
3.
4.
5.
6.
7.
8.
9.
10.

Say it out loud. "I can learn to swim." "I will pass this course." "I will get a job."

Do you really want to be happy, or are you going to sit back and watch the world go by? If you want to turn your life around, you can do it. Start by turning your mind around. Remember. Say to the obstacle: "Be thou Removed."

Saying: *I believe. I believe. I believe.*

9

I Can't Take It Any More

Seventeen-year-old Maria took twenty valiums. It was her second attempt at suicide. This one was successful. Her troubles all started after she was out sick from school for a month. She had trouble making up the work, in spite of the tutors her parents hired to help her. She begged her parents to let her repeat the semester instead of trying to make up the work, but they refused. They told her to do what she was "supposed" to do. But she couldn't. So she took what seemed to her to be the only escape from her troubles.

What happens when you just *can't* do what people tell you you're supposed to do, when the pressure becomes too much? Is Maria's solution the answer? No. There are many things Maria could have done to help herself, and I hope this chapter will give you some useful tips on handling pressure.

As a teenager, in spite of what many adults believe—

that all you have to think about is having fun—you have a load of responsibilities. First of all, you have schoolwork. Then you have demands being made upon you by your parents. They probably expect you not only to excel in school but to help with household chores and maybe to get an after-school job, too. Then there are the pressures you put on yourself. If you involve yourself in too many after-school activities, you may find that there's not enough time to fit them all in. You want to do better in your sport, you want to be more popular, you think you should lose weight, etc. Some of you have money pressures, sometimes concerning necessities—how to pay for college—or things that seem like necessities—how to find the money to dress like the other kids dress—or even outright luxuries—how to afford that new stereo or car. Then there is the pressure of decisions you must make about your future: Which colleges will you apply to? Will you get in? Which will you choose if you get in to them all?

Finally, there are pressures that life itself brings, especially those resulting from change: you go to a new school, your parents get divorced, your father loses his job, etc. Even the holidays bring with them a kind of pressure, a pressure to be happy because you're "supposed to be happy." What can we do about all this pressure? Is it always a bad thing?

– THE DIFFERENCE BETWEEN GOOD PRESSURE AND BAD PRESSURE –

Good pressure is just the right amount of push being exerted on you. It is good pressure that makes you do your homework at night and reminds you to show up for lacrosse practice, that gets you out of bed at night when you've forgotten to brush your teeth, that forces you to do those last two bench reps of the bench press. Without pressure of any kind, we'd be in trouble.

Bad pressure is the kind that overloads you—makes you feel as if you can't cope with all of the demands being made upon you. When you feel bad pressure you think, "I can't do this. There's not time, I'll never learn this," etc. It's a scary feeling and it can send you into a panic.

Simply put, good pressure is just the right amount of responsibility for you. It's pressure within the comfort zone. Bad pressure, on the other hand, is pressure you cannot live with, that makes you feel as though you're going to collapse under its weight.

If you are living under too much pressure you've probably been sending out a lot of messages to people around you. But maybe no one has been listening. Instead of giving in to the pressure (driving a car eighty miles an hour, escaping through drugs or alcohol, or killing yourself) why not learn how to take the pressure off?

– TAKING THE PRESSURE OFF –

SCHOOL PRESSURE

Let's tackle each pressure individually. Schoolwork is an ever-present threat to most teenagers. There's always that one teacher who's giving you a hard time. If this is the case, don't just wait around for things to change, or meet hostility with hostility. Sixteen-year-old Don says,

> I had this teacher who was always picking on me and marking me lower than he should have. At first I was so angry I wouldn't even speak to him about it, but then I decided to keep bugging him about his unfair attitude. After a while he lightened up, and I got to

know his ways, too. At least I didn't have to be the "wrong one" all the time.

If talking to your teacher doesn't work, don't be afraid to talk to the teacher's supervisor, who is usually the department chairperson. Explain your situation to the supervisor and ask for either a class change or a conference involving you, the supervisor, and the teacher. You'd be surprised how well this works. Once a teacher realizes how you feel and how determined you are to right the situation, he or she will pay special attention to treating you fairly in the future. The best part of taking this form of action is that you will no longer be alone in a no-win situation. You have gotten a more objective third party involved.

If you don't get any satisfaction from this effort, bring your parent to school and have your parent speak first to the teacher and then to the supervisor. Finally, if the teacher still gives you a problem, your parent can demand a class change for you.

What do you do when you can't seem to pass a course or to get your grades up to satisfactory level? Before you ask to have the course dropped or before you simply decide to go to summer school to make it up, you owe it to yourself to try this:

Invest fifteen extra minutes every night in that subject. Re-read your class notes, underlining important facts. Then re-read sections of your textbook. Call up a friend to help with any parts you don't understand. And if you don't have a friend who's good in the subject, then ask for help from somebody who seems smart in class, even if you barely know each other. You'd be surprised how flattering this can be, and how generous people sometimes are when you make them feel good about themselves. Put yourself in that position—wouldn't you help? Whenever you have a question that is unanswered, write it down and ask it the next day in class. Or, if you're too embarrassed to ask your questions during class sessions, speak to your teacher after class. You can also request tutoring.

Finally, try to participate in classroom discussions each day. Doing this forces you to get involved in the subject and it usually elevates you in the eyes of the teacher. He or she will be more willing to help you if it looks as if you're trying.

At first you may feel like a phony—just playing a game of pretense to pass a course. But after a while, you may surprise yourself by getting genuinely interested in the subject once you start to understand it. The payoff will come when your mark goes up by at least ten to twenty points.

If you've tried all of this and you still can't get a better mark, say to yourself, "I tried my best and that's all anyone can ask." And then—lay off yourself. If you have to repeat the course in summer school or next semester, fine. Failing grades make you feel awful. But they're definitely not worth dying over. And, if your parents refuse to understand, you have to convince them—as you convince yourself—to lay off. Even if they won't stop kicking you, *you* must stop kicking you.

What can you do about the general pressure you feel whenever a test is coming up? The best way to defuse this explosive situation is to prepare for the test as you go along. Think "preparation" each day as you sit in class and as you do your homework. Concentrate. If you will just give the matter at hand your full attention now, it will be that much easier when you're asked to reproduce the material on a test. Think of it this way: if you're sitting in a classroom for forty-five minutes anyway, you might as well use the time to prepare for the upcoming tests. There's nothing much else you can do with the time anyway. Think of all the pressure you'll be saving yourself later if you concentrate now.

PARENTAL PRESSURE

Parents put a lot of pressure on their teenagers—especially when it comes to doing well in school. What do you do if your parents insist that you remain in the advanced program when you just can't keep up with the work? Seventeen-year-old Raymond says,

> Get out! If you know you can't take it anymore, that's the only thing to do. I did that and now I'm in the top 15 in my graduating class. Before I wouldn't have even made the top 100. My mother didn't want me to drop advanced class and at first I felt guilty, but I see now that I did the right thing. Sometimes you just have to do what's best for you. It's better than cracking up, isn't it?

If your parents give you a hard time about dropping an advanced course, why not make a deal with them: you'll study all week and try your best to get an 85 or better on a given honors course test, and if you still don't get it, that's a sign that you should drop out. Then, of course, you must keep your part of the bargain and study hard. But if you really can't make the grade and you *have* studied, you should be allowed to drop an advanced class if you feel strongly about doing so.

The most important thing is to keep talking to your parents. If at first they don't get the message about how much pressure you are feeling and they lay a guilt trip on you about bad marks or whatever, then you'll just have to try again. Tell them you can't take it any more—if that's really how you feel. Today, parents are becoming more aware of the many demands being made on teenagers (thanks in part to the media, who have given a lot of publicity to teenage suicides).

Finally, if your parent still continues to pressure you, you must learn to say to yourself: "That's your problem, not mine." Maybe your parent is trying to realize an unfulfilled dream through you. Maybe he or she is counting on you to "make it," where he or she failed. Your parent may be living through you. If that's the case, throw off the burden. It's not yours. As I said in another context: Don't claim it.

There are many reasons for well-meaning parents overloading their teenagers with responsibilities. Some do it out of necessity; two working parents with financial worries may need a built-in babysitter, cook, and housecleaner. Other parents think it's important to teach their children what "the real world is like," as they express it. They may demand that you take on an after-school job even when you don't feel you can cope with the loss of study time, and don't want to cut down on your social life or give up any of your after-school activities, like sports.

If you think your parents simply don't realize how much pressure you are under, try writing them a letter explaining how you feel. Show them a chart of your daily routine so that they can see what you're dealing with. A typical twenty-four hour day might look something like this:

6:30 A.M.	Wake up and dress for school.
7:30–8:00	Travel to school.
8:30–3:00	School.
3:00–3:30	Travel home from school.
3:30–4:00	Straighten up the house.
4:00–4:30	Pick up sister at nursery school.
4:30–5:30	Get dinner ready.
5:30–6:30	Have dinner.
6:30–7:00	Do dishes.
7:00–8:30	Do homework.
8:30–9:00	Prepare clothing, take shower, etc.

| 9:00–10:30 | Free time. |
| 10:30–6:30 | Sleep. |

Your own schedule will, of course, be different, but if yours also has little space for breathing time, your parents may get the message once they see it in writing.

If that doesn't work and you're still stuck with that tight schedule, try to learn to cut corners. Maybe you could get some homework done on the bus going to and from school. Try inviting a friend along when you have to perform some household task. Having a friend in the kitchen with you as you prepare dinner, for example, can make the chore seem more like fun than work. Comfort yourself with thoughts about the holidays coming up, the summertime, and best of all, the future—when you will make your own schedule.

The surprising thing is that, if you get used to having such a crazy schedule as a teenager, you'll find as an adult that you'll be able to do twice or three times as much in a day as most people—and you may not want to slow down. The more you can pack into it, the more exciting life can be. And once you've formed the habit of using every minute wisely, you'll find that time stretches, and you have more of it for work *and* play.

SELF PRESSURE

Sometimes parents aren't the ones who are putting the pressure on—sometimes you're doing it to yourself. That can be the worst kind of pressure, but also the easiest to cure, since you have all the control.

A typical situation teenagers create for themselves is an overload of sports and other after-school activities. Seventeen-year-old Jason says,

Last year I was into piano, drums, bowling, basketball, baseball, hockey, karate, and quiz team. I felt pressed for time no matter what I did, I didn't want to give any of them up. I loved them all, but I let bowling go when the season ended, and I gave up karate because when I thought about it I didn't need it any more, and I could always go back when I'm 21. I also dropped the quiz team because that was taking up a lot of my time.

Jason evaluated his priorities so that he could decide which activities were most important to him—even though he "loved them all."

If you find yourself overloaded with activities, you may have to do the same thing. Like Jason, you can remind yourself that there are some sports or other activities that you can always take up next year or at a later time in your life. As the late Bernard Malamud once said, "Life is long." Why try to cram everything into a short period and ruin your joy? Space it out and let yourself breathe and enjoy life. Anyway, if you have to make a choice, it's better to do a few things well than a lot of things poorly.

Sometimes, however, you feel you're doing poorly in a sport (or other activity) even when time is not the problem. If so, speak to the coach or the teacher and ask for some advice. The coach may be able to give you some tips on how to improve. But the other reason to ask for specific feedback is that often you're being too hard on yourself, and you may need to hear that from the expert. For example, if you tell your karate teacher that you don't think you're doing well, the response may be something like, "That's not true at all. I've noticed a great improvement in your self-confidence since you began."

There are a host of other pressures you may inflict on yourself that are related to personal appearance and popularity. But once you've done your best to "work with what you have" as discussed in chapter 2, you have to get off your own back and accept yourself—and your limitations. If you like yourself, others will be drawn to you. There's no need to demand of yourself that you be the most popular or the best-looking in your school. As a matter of fact, that's not always so easy either. Fourteen-year-old Simone says,

Everyone thinks it's so great to be good looking, but I'm getting sick and tired of people hating me before they even get to meet me. They assume I'm stuck up just because of my looks. I'm always having to prove myself—that I'm not a cold———. Then there's the problem of my best friend. No matter who my best friend has been I've always had to play myself down and pretend that the guys we meet were interested in her when I knew they were after me. I would always be so relieved when a guy really took an interest in my friend. That would take the pressure off me.

You know, the worst part of it all is, there's no one you can tell this to. If you start talking about how it's a problem to be too good looking, forget it. They'll really hate you.

The truth is, nobody gets away from the pain of living. Nobody "has it made." It may seem so from a distance, but if you had to exchange lives with someone who you think gets all the breaks, you might be surprised to find yourself begging to have your old life back. The way I see it, your problems may be difficult, but they're tailor-made for you. If you couldn't handle them, they wouldn't be given to you. The fact that you're reading this chapter shows that you're interested in overcoming your pressures. Therefore you *will* overcome them.

DECISION PRESSURE

How can you deal with making major decisions like—What do you want to do with your life? Which college should you attend? Where will you get the money for college?

We've already discussed finding your goals in life. Your choice of a college may be related to those goals. For example, if you want to go to medical school, you should try to go to a school with a good pre-med program. If you're good with your hands and not much interested in academic subjects, you may want to find a good vocational school and forget about college, or just make a two-year junior college commitment. Your guidance counselor at school should be able to help you with decisions like this. The most important thing is planning ahead. If you *are* college bound, make sure you apply to several schools—a couple that are your top choices, and a few others as fallbacks in case you don't get in to the first choice. Even though it's a lot of work applying to several schools, it's better to be accepted into too many than too few—or none. You can always eliminate the less desirable ones if you get in everywhere.

The decision as to which college you should go to will be further narrowed down for you by your high school average, your S.A.T. scores, and the financial situation of your parents. Remember, though, if you don't get in to the college you wanted most, you can always apply again after one year at another college, as long as you do well.

Maybe the biggest thing that worries you is whether or not you should go away to college or continue to live at home and choose a school nearby. You and your parents will be the final judge of this, of course, but I think it's a good idea to go away if you have the choice. Going away to school provides a perfect intermediate state between being completely protected by your family and being completely on your own in the world. At college you can be very independent, but still not alone. Not only do you have your schoolmates, but there's an administration whose job it is to care for you and provide guidance and services for you.

The best part of going away is what happens after you graduate. You'll be used to living apart from your family by then, and it will be easier to go out on your own. If you stay home and go to a nearby college, however, it's harder to move out of the "nest." The longer you stay, the harder it is to leave. You may get spoiled by the comforts of home and end up still living with "Momma" at the age of twenty-five. I don't think that's good for you. I understand that many parents hate to see their children leave, but it's in your best interest to become independent as soon as possible. Your parents will get over their loss very quickly—especially when they see that they didn't really lose you at all. In fact relationships with parents often improve once you are not living with them.

Getting money for college is hard but not impossible. You can apply for scholarships (see your guidance counselor), or you can get a low-interest student loan. Many colleges have work-study programs or grants, depending upon your family's financial position. Of course, if you want to go to Harvard or Yale, or one of the other really expensive schools and your parents can't afford the tuition, you should think hard about whether it's really worth it to you to be saddled with tens of thousands of dollars in debt once you graduate. Don't get hung up on a fancy name and prestige. There are plenty of good schools that aren't in the Ivy League. Ask older friends about their colleges.

No matter what the financial situation of your family, you will be able to go to some university if you explore all the possibilities and are willing to work part-time to help put yourself through.

FINANCIAL PRESSURE

What about financial pressures in general? Many teen-agers want the latest in fashion or an expensive stereo system or a fine car, but the family can't afford to give them such luxuries. If you are in this position you may feel deprived or frustrated. What should you do?

After looking at your schedule, decide whether or not you can handle an after-school job. Then evaluate your priorities. Is a car worth the time you'll have to give up to earn money for it, or would you rather just hang around with friends? Do you really need a new stereo enough to justify giving up after-school activities? Are expensive clothes more important than sports? Only you can answer these questions, because everyone's priorities are different. You might want to list all the things that are important to you now, and then put them in order so that you know which to sacrifice, if any. Don't forget saving money for college, if your parents can't afford to pay all your tuition.

If you organize your time you'll be surprised to find that you can get more done than you ever thought you could. But there are still only twenty-four hours in the day. If you're having trouble fitting everything in, keep track of how you spend a typical school day, beginning with waking up in the morning and ending (I hope) with eight hours of sleep at night, remembering to include mealtimes, transportation to and from places, and all the other things that eat up time without your even being aware of it. Make a separate schedule for Saturday and Sunday. You may be surprised by the results. For example, there are time blocks which can be used more efficiently. Perhaps you've been spending twenty hours a week watching television. Those twenty hours could be used for sports, or studying, or working at an after-school job. Maybe you've been spending ten hours a week on the telephone. If you cut it down to three, you have seven hours to use for something higher on your priority list.

Once you've figured out how you actually do spend time, make a plan for how you want to spend your time. Then you can check each thing off after you've done it. It makes you feel good inside to know that you have accomplished what you planned to do. It makes you feel in control of your life. Feeling in control takes a lot of the pressure off.

THE PRESSURE OF CHANGE

There are pressures that have nothing to do with organizing your time, and the pressure of change is one of them. Whether the change is good or bad, change always brings tension. One of the hardest things for most teenagers to do is to get used to a new school. At first it seems as if you'll never learn where everything is. You feel lost and alone. Everyone else seems to be in a clique and you feel left out. You may even get so depressed you think of cutting school every morning when you get up. But think of it this way: You've already been through the scariest change of all, which was going to school in the first place. You were just a little kid then, much less able to cope with big changes, and being in school was terrifying. But you did it. And after a while, you felt quite comfortable in your school. Most of you have already made the change from elementary school to junior high school, and that wasn't easy at first either, but you did get used to it. Some of you have moved from junior high to high school, and you know that you even got used to that.

The key is to remember that time changes all things. Before you know it, the new will become the old. Your frightened feelings will disappear as time goes on. Keep in mind, "this too shall pass."

Any family change can be a threat. If your parents get divorced, it seems like the end of the world. If your father has left the house you feel terrible. There's an empty space. You keep wanting things to go back to the way they used to be. You spend a lot of time thinking about why it happened, and how it "should be." Don't do that. It's a waste of energy. Instead, allow yourself to be sad because you have lost your daily contact with one parent, but realize that you didn't lose that parent. Your father will come and visit. He still loves you. (I say "father," because usually the kids stay with the mother. But the reverse is of course true, too.) Whatever happened is not your fault. It's between two adults—your parents. Think of all the other teenagers whose parents are divorced. Talk to some of your friends. There will be quite a few who have divorced parents; they can assure you that you'll get used to it and that your life will eventually go back to normal.

Other changes in the family situation can make you feel pressure for a while, too. If your mother starts working, or your father loses his job—or even if your family won the lottery—there will be pressure until things settle down. Keep telling yourself, "this feeling is temporary. I'll get used to the new—and it will soon be old." Then you won't panic. By talking to yourself that way, you calm yourself down and you take the pressure off.

HOLIDAY PRESSURE

Even though the holidays are supposed to be a happy time, they can cause major depression. Why? You're expected to be happy, after all, if it's Christmas, for example. But what if you don't happen to be feeling joyful? The result may be that you feel guilty. It's the same as when people tell you that these are the best years of your life.

That puts pressure on you to be happy. And when you feel pressure to be happy, then it's harder than ever to feel what you think you should feel. You start comparing this Christmas to last Christmas or some other Christmas when things were going better for you. You may recall an ex-boyfriend or girlfriend who shared the holidays with you and begin lamenting the fact that this year you have no one special to celebrate with.

Comparing one year to another when it comes to holidays is always a trap. Although the holidays come with regularity, the ups and downs of life don't obey any calendar, so you may have to celebrate Christmas when it's the last thing in the world you feel like doing because you just failed trig, or broke up with your steady, or found out you didn't get in to college on that early admissions program you applied to.

Instead of feeling bad because things aren't going your way, try to forget your troubles for the moment and just enter into the fun of the season as well as you can. Enjoy the holiday atmosphere, the sight of the many Santa Clauses in the streets and in the department stores. Get into the excitement of shopping. Surprise someone who is not expecting a gift from you.

Spend time with your family this year. Enjoy the warmth and happiness you have at home. Soon enough you'll have left home and may not be able to spend all your holidays with your family. Learn to treasure the time you have with them now.

Don't isolate yourself. Call up old friends. The holidays are a good time to get together with people you haven't seen in a long time. Give a "tree trimming" party, for example. Each person brings an ornament for the tree. You might even add that each person must bring a friend, too. That's a good way to meet new people.

One of the best ways to make yourself happy around the holidays is to do something kind for someone who is less fortunate than you. Volunteer to help with the local nursery school party. Go Christmas caroling in a hospital on Christmas Eve. Or get together with a bunch of friends and go caroling in your neighborhood. Your songs are sure to put a smile on even the saddest face—which would in turn put a smile on yours.

Sixteen-year-old Monica says,

Last Christmas Eve I was so depressed because I had broken up with my boyfriend. This group from school was going Christmas caroling in Harlem Hospital. I didn't want to go, but then I thought, "If I stay home I'll only think about him and get more depressed." I met the group and we went to the hospital together. I'll never forget it. There was this old black man. He looked so sad and lonely. When we got to his bed and started singing, "Joy to the World," he sat up on one elbow and looked surprised. Then we broke into "Jingle Bells." By now he was smiling, you could see all of his teeth. He really looked happy. By the time we finished with "Silent Night," he had tears in his eyes. I don't know what happened, but as we sang at each bed, the person would come alive. When I went home that night I was so happy I didn't know what to do with myself. I was smiling at people and I felt like kissing everybody. It was so beautiful to see how happy those people were—just over a few songs we sang for them. The funny part is, I forgot all about my depression. When I remembered how sad I was, the whole thing seemed so small to me then. The new feeling had taken over completely.

So make it your business to do something for someone else. Say "I love you" to someone with a word or a deed.

Watch your own heart leap with joy as you do. Your depression will disappear.

In conclusion, no matter what kind of pressure you're feeling, there *is* something you can do about it. You don't have to depend upon others to save you, and you don't have to escape by running out on life itself. Remember, if the pressure is too much, take action. Throw off the burden. It's better to give something up, to get rid of it, than to give up your life.

Saying: *This too shall pass.*

10

Witches, Queens, Princes, and Don Juans

Have you met any of the above-mentioned characters? This is a chapter all about depressing situations involving the opposite sex.

It really hurts when you like someone a lot who has no interest in you at all. It's also depressing when you're going out with someone who suddenly begins to act "coldly" toward you but you don't know why. It gets worse: Sometimes you *do* know why—it's because that person no longer wants to be with you. It's awful when someone you've been seeing forever wants to break up with you. Another real killer is when your boyfriend or girlfriend is seeing other people behind your back. And equally devastating is when something you did behind closed doors is suddenly the hottest gossip in town. Or when you've been pushed into doing something you don't want to do, and you feel used.

- UNRETURNED LOVE -

No matter how depressing your romantic situation is, if you think logically you can prevent yourself from going to pieces. Let's start with the problem of liking someone who couldn't care less about you.

Fifteen-year-old Wendy says,

There was this guy, Joe, in our crowd that I would always joke around with. I liked him more than as a friend but he didn't seem to notice, so I told him I had a dream about him, and I started telling him the details. He gave me this look and said, "Keep dreaming." After that I couldn't even look at him.

Wendy is embarrassed because she exposed her feelings and her feelings were not returned. In fact, she was rejected as a girlfriend—but not as a person. Joey liked her fine until he understood that she wanted more than friendship from him. Then, probably because he was embarrassed, he said something cruel.

If someone of the opposite sex isn't interested in you, think of a time when you also had to say no to someone who was interested in you romantically. When I asked Wendy, she remembered rejecting a boy and making him feel almost as bad as Joey made her feel, though she hadn't meant to do so. Wendy says:

This guy Steve, started writing me letters and asking friends to tell me that he liked me. At first I took it as a joke, but it wasn't. Eventually, I had to tell him to his face that I wasn't interested in him. His face got all red and he walked away. I felt bad but I had to get him off my back.

Wendy was rejected romantically by Joey, Steve was rejected romantically by Wendy, and Joey has no doubt been rejected romantically by someone else. In fact, every person in the world will be rejected romantically by someone, and probably more than once or twice. But that's not because of any flaws they have. The fact is, we are all very complicated. There's no predicting who will work together romantically and who won't (as you know if you've ever tried to fix a friend up with a blind date). We have so many complex personality traits and psychological needs that it's really a miracle that two people ever find each other at all.

But they do. The same person who is rejected romantically by someone will be adored by someone else. Steve and Wendy will have more than one person fall in love with them—and so will you. And eventually you'll fall in love with one of them, too. Sometimes it just takes a while for it to happen simultaneously. You have to be patient—hard as that is.

Keep in mind that when you try to get the attention of someone and that person doesn't respond, it's not because of anything that's wrong with you. You're just not that person's type, the same way someone else was not yours.

How can you keep yourself from wasting time being sad and depressed over the fact that you can't get the one you love to love you back? Think to yourself, "What good is a one-sided love affair? I need someone who is crazy about me." When you think about how indifferent that person is toward you, let it turn you off. Learn to get excited only about people who show a spark of interest in you, too! Instead of getting depressed, get angry enough to walk around with a devil-may-care attitude and make up your mind to magnetize someone into your life—someone who will appreciate what you have to offer.

– LACK OF COMMUNICATION –

What about when you do have a relationship, but your boyfriend or girlfriend is angry over something and refuses to talk to you? You can become very depressed. You wonder what you did wrong. You start imagining all sorts of things.

Fourteen-year-old Jenny says,

Dave hung up on me three times. I had no idea why he was mad. I started thinking it was because I had jokingly said "drop dead," when his friends were around. Later he told my friend that he was mad because we were going to visit her good-looking cousins. Now why couldn't Dave have told me that in the first place and saved me all that aggravation?

Jenny dealt with her problem very sensibly by asking her friend to do some checking up. But that method might take a while and while you're waiting you'll be in pain. What else can you do? Sometimes there's not much you can do, and you have to know when to give up.

If this kind of situation comes up a lot with your boyfriend or girlfriend and you find that he or she just won't open up to you but keeps shutting you out, you need to ask yourself if it's worth staying in the relationship. Unless you have thick skin you might be better off finding someone who is more open. As a teenager you have enough troubles in your life: school, parents, appearance, etc. Why add pain to your life in an area that should give pleasure? Shouldn't your relationship with your boyfriend/girlfriend be one of the happiest things in your life? If it's not, it's more trouble than it's worth.

Learning to move out of unpleasant relationships now is good practice for the future. It can prevent you from marrying someone who will doom you to a life of silent misery.

– BREAKING UP WHEN YOU DON'T WANT TO –

When things start to cool down on one side of the relationship, and it's not your side (but there doesn't seem to be anything you can do about it), you sense that something is wrong and you spend most of your time worrying about breaking up.

Fifteen-year-old Jackie says:

> I really liked George, and in the beginning he treated me like gold. Then he started to act as if I wasn't even there. It was such a letdown. Then he started picking fights with me over stupid things. Finally, I told him, "I can't stand you any more. It's over." He seemed glad. I was so depressed all week.

George wasn't fair to Jackie. He made her do the "dirty work," so to speak. He wanted to break up with her but he didn't have the courage to face her with the news so he became cold and then cruel.

Jackie got the message. But instead of falling into the trap of being forced to break up with George (after all, she didn't want to break up, he did) she should have said:

> George, you've been treating me differently for the last few weeks. I get the feeling you want to break up, am I right?

By confronting George in a nonaccusatory way, Jackie would be giving him a chance to be honest and say,

"You're right. . . ." This way Jackie wouldn't have to suffer twice as much. It's bad enough to suffer because someone you love breaks up with you, but it's twice as bad when that person tricks you into doing the breaking up. That leaves you confused and frustrated. It also leaves a feeling of loose ends. You keep saying to yourself, "Maybe I made a mistake. Maybe he didn't really want to break up, and it was all my fault."

It's so much better to bring things out in the open and make the other person come clean with you. This way you can end it in your own mind. You'll know it's really over, and that will free you to move on to other romantic interests. Don't think that there's anything wrong with *you* just because things didn't work out this time. Remember the story of Wendy and Joey. People fall in and out of love for no particular reason. (Think of some of the odd couples you've seen.) If George doesn't like you, Tom may be wild about you. That's what the dating game is all about—finding out who is and is not compatible for the long run.

– CHEATING –

The ultimate downer can be when you find out that your boyfriend/girlfriend is cheating on you. Seventeen-year-old Darryl says,

I found out my girl was cheating on me all along. I felt like killing him and then killing her, but it wasn't worth it. I care more about myself.

Why do people cheat on each other? Most people who cheat want the best of both worlds. They want to have a guarantee that no one goes out with their sweetheart, but at the same time, they want to be sure not to miss out on any exciting person who comes along. In short, they want to "have their cake and eat it too."

Of course it isn't fair for someone to treat you that way, to cheat on you, but you should consider a few points.

In my opinion, teenagers are really too young to limit themselves to a one-to-one relationship. Your teenage years are the time when you're supposed to be exploring different possibilities. It would be much better to make an agreement with the person you love that you two are going steady, but if either one of you wants to go out with someone else, it's okay—so long as you tell each other. I realize that you're probably saying, "No way" because the thought of your boyfriend or girlfriend going out with someone else bothers you. Well, if that's so, you may have to pay the price of being cheated on, or maybe even cheating yourself. Remember—cheating during the teenage years is not really cheating. It's just being a teenager.

If you're going steady, and your steady cheats on you, try to think of it this way. Your steady loves you so much that he or she didn't want to take the chance of losing you—but at the same time your steady is being very unfair to you. There's no need to hate the person, just set the relationship in order. Make it clear that now you will both be free to see others. But if you really believe that you want an exclusive relationship with someone, then you'd better break up with the person who cheated on you and try your luck somewhere else.

Whatever you do, don't fall into the trap of categorizing all people of the opposite sex as untrustworthy. And don't try to take your revenge on the next person who comes along. It isn't fair to the rest of the gender. Be an independent thinker. Take each case as it comes.

Think of it this way: If you're a true-blue person, you're probably not the only one in the world—there must be someone else out there who is also forthright and honest.

Make up your mind to find that person. Never let bad experiences in the past poison your future.

– LETTING GO OF A LONG TERM RELATIONSHIP –

A very painful and potentially murderously depressing situation occurs when you break up with someone you've been going with for a long time. That person was a major part of your life, and when he or she goes, there's an empty space. You feel lonely.

Your mistake is that you don't believe that space will be filled by something or someone else, but it will. In time you'll make different use of the hours you spent with that person. It will happen naturally. You'll have more time for your friends. You'll go to parties and dances. You'll start working on the school paper. You'll meet new people. It's inevitable. And one of these days you'll think, "I haven't been missing ——— at all. When did I stop?"

Some of you may believe that you'll never find another boyfriend/girlfriend who will be the same. And you're right. But you'll find someone different—better for you—somewhere down the line.

But nothing I've said is meant to underestimate your pain. Don't feel bad about feeling bad. It's healthy for you to "mourn" your loss. Everyone needs to mourn a lost love. Get it all out of your system. Have a good cry. Write sad poems. Take long walks. But then, one day, let the sun shine in your life. Say to yourself, "I'm ready for the future." And you will be. Now that you've finished with a relationship that wasn't going anywhere, anything can happen.

Every so often you may still catch yourself daydreaming

of that person and crying. You may picture how perfect the two of you were together. The only thing I can suggest to you when that happens is that you play another movie in your mind. Think about the bad times—the times you fought and said vicious things to each other—and for now forget the good times. Think of the worst thing your ex did to you. Dwell on it. Realize that it wasn't all roses after all. If it had been, you'd still be together.

I've saved the best for last. What do you do about someone who kisses and tells—to the point where what happened behind closed doors is now being featured all over town?

– WHEN THEY KISS AND TELL –

Suppose you had a sexual experience that you now regret. To make matters worse, now the whole school knows about it and you feel like never coming out of your house again.

The key here is that nobody actually saw anything. There were no video cameras recording the action. Don't let your imagination, embarrassment, and guilt run away with the situation. You can regain control. Since no one can prove that what this person is saying is true, as far as you're concerned, NOTHING HAPPENED. Your attitude should be, "Let 'em talk." If anybody asks you about it say, "I heard," and laugh. Then say, "He must be doing some pretty funny drugs. I think he's hallucinating" (or something of the kind).

The point is, make a big joke out of it and the tale-teller will look like a fool. You have something else on your side. Most people are suspicious of those who go around bragging about their sexual exploits. People are reluctant to believe them. Often it's the guys who aren't sexually experienced who feel pressure to make up stories to prove that they are. So you see, you really have nothing to worry about. As long as it wasn't filmed, NOTHING HAPPENED. The joke is on the bigmouth, not on you.

– BEING USED –

Now that we're on the subject of sex, let's talk about how people (mainly girls) sometimes get "used." There are two kinds of "using" when it comes to sex: planned and unplanned. "Planned" using is when the boy thinks ahead of time of tricks he can use to make a girl have sex with him. He will tell any lie, put on any act, as long as it gets him to the goal. Most using comes under the second category: unplanned using. As fourteen-year-old Eileen says,

> The boy doesn't think about how the girl feels when it comes to sex. He's only thinking of his own feelings. When you come to think of it, the girl isn't thinking about what the boy feels either. She's thinking of herself. I think at that age it's natural to forget about how the other one feels.

If this is true, a boy might push the sexual situation to the limit, thinking only of his own needs. The girl who gives in even though she isn't ready to get involved with that boy sexually later feels lonely and guilty. Lonely because she might have been expecting love in return for sex while the boy was merely enjoying the physical moment of passion, and guilty because she has done something she didn't really want to do.

When two people have sex, if one is looking for love and the other is just looking for a good time, the love seeker is going to get hurt.

– RIGHT AND WRONG SEX –

There are other ways to misuse sex. Some teenagers are still not sure of who they are. They suffer from low self-esteem, they don't feel as if they are worth very much. They go into sexual relationships to fill the gap—to try to get the feeling of personal worth. They mistakenly believe that the momentary pleasure of the sexual act will somehow become a permanent reassurance that they are really okay. This is why some fellows (and even some girls these days) look at a sexual experience as a conquest, another "notch in the belt," so to speak. What these teenagers don't realize is they'll never get a true feeling of self-esteem from sex. Self-esteem comes, as discussed before, from building up a good reputation with one's self. Having sex with a lot of people is probably one of the *worst* ways to do this, because all that bed hopping will give you a bad reputation with yourself. You'll end up feeling worse than ever. (And you may contract AIDS or V.D. in the bargain.)

The only way to get yourself out of such a depressing situation is to admit to yourself what is really going on. Say to yourself, "Okay, I've been looking for something good in the wrong place." Then start working on your self-esteem the right way. Save your sexual experiences for when you are ready to give of yourself and to truly love your sexual partner. Remember, if you're having sex for any reason other than love, something is wrong.

You can't always be sure it's right even if you do love someone. Maybe that person doesn't feel the same way about you. Then you'll be depressed later. Sex is for the mature. When immature people engage in sex they're bound to eventually become depressed because they cannot handle the many emotions that come with sex. They get all mixed up and confused.

If you want to avoid sexually depressing situations, I say wait until you're mature to start having sexual relationships. How mature? Very mature.

Saying: *Another love will come along*.

11

Tragedies of a Life-Changing Nature

Let's face it. The worst thing that can happen to you short of your own death is the death of your mother or father. Your parents are so much a part of you that if one of them dies, it feels as if a part of you has died, too. You're left with an emptiness that seems unbearable.

When you're a child and a teenager need for your parents is at its greatest. You depend on them not only for love and moral support but for the basics: food and shelter. Small wonder that the death of a parent rates 100 points on the stress scale designed to measure the amount of pressure experienced as a result of various life changes. (In contrast, the same scale rates death of a close family member at 63, moving at 26, and changing friends at 18).[1]

------

[1]David Elkind, *The Hurried Child* (Massachusetts Reading: Addison-Wesley Publishing Company, 1981), pp. 162–63.

When your parent is suddenly taken out of your life, and you know that the loss is permanent, you feel three immediate emotions: loneliness, guilt, and anger. Loneliness because you miss your parent and keep wishing that you could have just one more chance to be with that parent, and guilt because you begin to think of all the "bad" things you said or did to that parent. You regret not telling your parent how much you loved him or her before it was too late. In addition, you feel horrible about the times when, after a particularly vicious argument with your parent, you may have thought, "I wish you were dead." You also feel angry because you feel abandoned by your parent.

– DEALING WITH LONELINESS AFTER THE DEATH OF A PARENT –

The first step in coping with the loss of your parent is coming to terms with the loneliness—the empty space in your life. Before you do anything else, let yourself grieve. This involves crying whenever and wherever and to whomever you please. Don't try to "tough it out," and hold back your emotions. Even the most hardened criminal would sympathize with your tears if he knew you were crying over the death of your parent.

Part of grieving is talking about your parent and your feelings to others. Talk to whomever you feel like talking to—family, friends, teachers, counselors. It doesn't matter who, so long as it's someone you're comfortable with and trust. Express your fears, regrets, sorrows. If you don't let yourself cry and talk, you'll drive the pain deep down into yourself where it will seethe and fester, only to reappear at a later time—and in an unhealthy way. You may find yourself overreacting to seemingly minor situations years later if you don't let yourself express your sorrow now. You may also find yourself in a continual and very long-lasting state of depression if you try to suppress your genuine pain.

Your parent is no longer with you physically, so you believe that he or she is gone, erased. That just isn't so. Your parent is as much a part of your life as ever, only now you have to depend upon your mind to feel your parent's presence. The many years you and your parent spent together have not disappeared. They are within you. They *are* you. Every experience the two of you shared has helped to make you who you are today. If you think hard, you can even imagine what advice your parent would give you if you have a certain problem. All you have to do is picture yourself sitting with your parent and having a conversation. Ask your parent what you should do in a situation that's troubling you. Soon you'll see your parent answering you and you'll know what he or she would advise. This isn't a made-up inner movie. You can do this because your parent really *is* a part of you. As a psychologist would say, you have internalized your parent. You can imagine your parent being there with you anytime you want. At these times you can tell your parent how much you miss and love him or her.

One of the most beautiful ways to experience your parent's presence again is in a dream. You may find yourself having many dreams in which your parent hugs you, comforts you, and encourages you. I've spoken to many teenagers who have lost a parent and each one can tell me of such a dream. Sixteen-year-old Sandy says,

My mother died when I was thirteen. I've had many dreams of her since then. The last dream I had of her was when she was saying to me: "I'm so glad to see you're going in the right direction and you're taking up nursing after all. Her eyes were so soft and wise and loving. When I woke up I felt good inside and it lasted for days—even weeks. It's like she's still with me—I can't exactly explain it.

But what if you don't have any dreams? Don't worry, you will. Your subconscious mind will bring that dream to you because of your continual thoughts about your parent. When a parent dies, it doesn't matter whether you're consciously thinking of him or her, because your subconscious mind is working on the loss—trying to come to terms with it.

One of the things that may worry you most is that you feel you can't remember exactly what your parent looked like. This happens to everyone who has lost someone he loves. One thing you might do to ease that fear is to make a photo album of your parent—perhaps focusing on pictures that remind you of all the good times you had together over the years. You will get a lot of pleasure from looking through that album.

One of the most tormenting aspects of losing a parent is the guilt you feel when that parent dies.

– GETTING RID OF GUILT –

You think of all the negative things you said or did to your parent and you torture yourself with the fact that now it's too late to change what happened.

First, you remember every smart answer you ever gave your parent. Then you think of the times you may have said, "I hate you," or even in a moment of rage wished that parent were dead. Every normal teenager feels momentary hatred toward a parent. You will recall that in chapter 5 we discussed how even parents express hatred toward their own children in moments of rage. But just as a parent doesn't *really* hate a child, it's not really your parent you hated when you blew up, but what the parent was saying or doing to you at that moment. Nevertheless, it's normal to wish you had the chance to say, "I'm sorry, Mommy, I really do love you," or "Forgive me, Daddy, for slamming the door in your face that day," and so on.

Do you think your parent would feel sorry for you if he or she could see how you are suffering now with all this guilt? Would he or she forgive you if you asked for forgiveness? Picture your parent sitting with you in a favorite place. See yourself saying all the things you would say if your parent were still alive. See your parent listening. Say it all and watch your parent forgive you and comfort you. Again, let me remind you: this is not just some made-up fantasy. The reason you can create such a picture in your mind is because that's who your parent was—and *is*. Accepting forgiveness from your parent is one way of keeping him or her alive in you, of being faithful to his or her memory. Accept that forgiveness. You know it's real. You know your parent wouldn't want you to suffer with guilt over problems you had with him or her in the past. You are forgiven. Enjoy the feeling of your loving, understanding parent forgiving you. Wherever your parent is, one thing is for sure. He or she is now above all petty grievances of the past. He or she sees the big picture now, and can afford to forgive all things.

Your mind may bring things up at the most unexpected times—things that happened between you and your parent. You may be in the middle of a hockey game and suddenly you'll get a flash of the time you hung up the phone on your mother and she worried about you all day. Talk to the mother you see in your mind when that happens. Tell her you're sorry about what you did. You'll feel better right away because you'll know that your mother has forgiven you and that she doesn't want to see you suffer.

Think of it this way—from your parent's point of view. The last thing your parent wanted to do was to die—to leave and not be able to take care of you. But it happened. Now that your parent is gone, he or she would hate to see you suffering over something that happened between you two in the past. Let your parent at least take care of you in this way now—let your parent forgive you. Wouldn't your parent be relieved to see you coping with his or her death. Wouldn't your parent be happy to see you treasuring the times you had together, and keeping his or her memory alive within you by talking to that memory whenever you feel in need of love or guidance?

Now that your parent is gone, it's up to you to make sure that all of the hard work he or she put into teaching you how to live is not wasted. Why not go out there and overcome every obstacle in your way. Be a success. DO it in memory of your parent. What better way could there possibly be of making your parent live on—than in your own words and deeds!

– DEALING WITH ANGER AFTER THE DEATH OF A PARENT –

You may not realize it on a conscious level, but you are probably feeling a good bit of anger over your parent's death. You may feel cheated. "Why did my dad have to go and desert me this way? It just isn't fair." You may resent the fact that now it will be impossible for your parent to fulfill the many promises he or she made to you. Of course, you know that it isn't your parent's fault that he or she died, but yet you feel that rage. So you take it out on life. "Life is just not fair, damn it." And you seethe in silent anger.

But anger finds ways out. You may have nightmares about your parent—ugly dreams in which your parent is cast in a cruel role or in a role in which he or she is being harmed. There may be a lot of violence—blood and gore—in these nightmares. Actually, from a psychological point of view, such nightmares can be considered healthy. They are the way your unconscious works out its anger and frustration. Although the nightmares are unpleasant and even terrifying, they help you to "get it out of your system," especially if you're someone who finds it difficult to open up to people and you've never been able to talk much about the death of your parent. The nightmare may be your only "vent," and it can save you from the buried anger that may be eating at you from within.

It's perfectly normal to feel angry and cheated and even resentful if a parent dies. Don't feel guilty about those feelings. Instead, admit them to yourself and realize that everyone who has lost a parent feels the same way.

Another tragedy that changes your life is when your parent is very sick.

– DEALING WITH FRUSTRATION OVER A SICK PARENT –

Fifteen-year-old Danny says,

I get so depressed when I visit my father in the hospital. I see him lying in bed so pale and skinny I want to cry—I can't stand to see him that way. The worst part is there's nothing I can do to get him better. The thing I do to keep from showing my depression to my father is talk about happy things. I ask him questions and offer him food.

When a parent is sick it's normal to suffer when you see the change in his or her physical condition. Danny wants to cry when he sees how pale and thin his father is. If he did cry, his father would understand and even be touched by it. That's one way for the two of them to get close during this painful time.

As Danny says, the worst part *is* the helplessness you feel. You can't make your parent better. However, you can make your parent's mind feel better, and here's how:

Whatever you do, don't run away because you can't stand to see your parent looking so bad. Force yourself to visit your parent in the hospital or to spend time with him or her at home. Nothing could be more comforting to a sick parent than the love and affection you can give.

Next, let your parent take the lead in talking—or being silent—about how he or she feels. Some people want to talk; others don't. Respect your parent's wishes either way. If your parent wants to talk about what will happen if he or she dies, then let yourself be drawn into the discussion. It will be good for both of you. By facing, instead of running away from, a possible reality, you and your parent will feel reassured. You can make plans together about what will happen if your parent dies. It's important for both of you to feel that he or she was a part of planning your future. And if your parent gets well, there was no harm done in preparing for the possibility of death. Talking about it doesn't make it happen. And not talking about it can't prevent it from happening. The most important thing for you both is to be close to each other and support each other at this sad, scary time. Whatever happens, the memories you'll keep of the closeness you shared will always be happy ones.

Also try to have as many talks with your parent as possible—talks that review all of the good times you had together. This will cheer your parent up and at the same time bring the two of you closer together. Let your parent talk about his or her own life in general. A deathly ill person needs to review his or her life, and unfortunately, too often, no one wants to listen. By listening you will not only comfort your parent but you will learn more about him or her and add to your collection of memories. You will also, of course, be giving your parent the most wonderful gift in the world—your love and understanding.

Do as many kind things for your parent as you can think of. Don't push away seemingly impulsive ideas such as bringing your parent a favorite dish from a particular restaurant, or writing a letter telling how much you love him or her, or bringing a single rose to the hospital on a visit. Maybe you think these things don't matter to a person who is really sick. But they do. They are beautiful reminders of the pleasures of life—and love. People want to enjoy whatever of life they can while they are still alive. So you should enjoy the fact that your parent is still alive, and that there are so many things you can do for your parent while there is time left.

These suggestions will probably have occurred to you anyway, but the problem is that most people are so shocked and depressed by serious illness that they don't take action on their thoughts. Force yourself to break through your state of semiparalysis and do what you know you should do. You'll find that each time you take action you'll feel a surge of energy return to you and you won't be as depressed. You'll still feel deep sorrow, but it will be a positive, healthy sorrow instead of a fearful, dreadful sorrow.

Sometimes, however, nothing you do seems able to make a difference. When a person is very sick, sometimes he or she cannot respond in any positive way to acts of kindness and love. Pain and medication may alter a personality. If your parent seems distant, irritable, or otherwise strange, don't take it personally. Realize that your parent is using all of his or her energy to stay alive. And don't stop trying. Even if your parent doesn't show any appreciation, you'd be amazed to know how much your efforts can mean to a sick person.

Finally, don't keep your sadness to yourself. Talk to other family members, friends, teachers, friends of the family, etc. Tell someone, anyone, that you are very worried because your mother is in the hospital, or because your father had an accident. No matter who you tell, that person will almost certainly show sympathy and understanding and make you feel better. Reach out to someone and you'll get comfort. Wouldn't you have a heart for someone whose parent was deathly ill? And someday you will have a chance to comfort others in the same situation. But now is your time to be comforted. Stop punishing yourself by forcing yourself to suffer alone. Take the comfort that you need now. It's there waiting for you. Even if you told a perfect stranger—say the person sitting next to you on a bus—"I'm so miserable. My mother is in the hospital. . . ."—that person would comfort you; that's how universal the pain of a sick mother or father is.

The death of a family member other than your parent—or of a good friend—can also be very painful. That person was a part of your life and now that part is missing. You must allow yourself time to mourn that death. Mourn and grieve as much as you feel like. There's no "proper" amount—so much for a sister, so much for an uncle, and so forth. If you were extremely close to that person, then it doesn't matter if he was your third cousin. He might as well have been your brother. Whatever your feelings are, they're right. Feelings don't lie, and they don't follow rules either. Accept them. Use all of the methods for dealing with pain that were discussed in the beginning of this chapter.

– DEALING WITH THE LOSS OF
A PET –

Fifteen-year-old Tama says,

Every time I think about my cat I get depressed. I really loved him. At nights I cry because I miss him so much. But I know it's ridiculous to care this much about an animal. So I don't let anyone know.

It's not silly at all to cry over the death of a pet. The two of you were friends. You had a relationship. The saying "a dog is a man's best friend," was coined for a good reason. Sometimes we can feel closer to our pets than we can to people. A pet always loves you, never judges or rejects you. A pet is always in the mood to play, and a pet is always there when you want company.

If you've lost a pet, try talking to someone else who has had the same experience. This person can understand and can make you see that the pain you feel is normal and real. You really do need time to mourn. In fact, some people feel so much pain over the loss of a pet that there are even therapists who specialize in pet "bereavement" (mourning).

After you've given yourself time to mourn the loss of your pet, plan to get another one. "It won't be the same," you say. Right. It will be different—and still great. Isn't it true that even parents who suffer the loss of a child will often have another baby to fill the empty space in their hearts? If people can do that with children, why not with pets?

There's no need to punish yourself by refusing to get another pet. Maybe you think it's being disloyal to the memory of your pet. Well, it isn't. It's a tribute to your love for your pet that you want another one. Studies have shown that widowed people who were the most happily married are the most likely to remarry. So don't feel guilty about wanting to be happy again with a new pet—it's normal.

There are other life-changing tragedies besides death.

– THE TRAGEDY OF AN UNWANTED PREGNANCY –

An unwanted pregnancy can scare you literally "to death."

I was fifteen when I got pregnant. This guy had forced himself on me but I never told anyone. Now that I knew I was pregnant I figured no one would believe my story. I thought about jumping off a roof to end it all. Finally I told my mother all about it and she believed me. It was too late to get an abortion so I had the baby and I gave it up for adoption. I think about that baby all the time, and it makes me sad, but now I have a wonderful boyfriend and we're getting married next May. I went through a lot of pain, and I still suffer when I think of the baby and wonder how she's doing—but I am happy in my life.

Nadeen, 19 years old.

It may seem like the end of the world if you're pregnant, but it isn't. Only you can make it the end of the world by giving in to that fear and panic and killing yourself. Remember, no matter what happens, if you stay alive, this too will pass, and then you can go on with your life.

No matter what you decide to do, don't kill yourself. You can have the child and raise it, or give it up for adoption, or you can decide not to have it, depending upon your personal feelings about abortion. This is a very difficult question and it's hard to know what is right. You may be deeply disturbed about taking the life of your unborn child, but *nothing* is worse than taking your own life. Then you kill a full grown person—yourself—*and* your unborn child. There really is life after pregnancy. Many other young women have faced this terrible dilemma, and found happiness afterwards, no matter what choice they made.

Remember, abortion is a personal matter. You have to make up your own mind how you feel about it. And choosing whether to raise your baby or give it up for adoption by people who will be better able to care for it is also a personal matter. Don't, however, try to make this decision all by yourself. It's too big a decision, and you're too upset. You must talk to an adult you trust and respect.

Don't forget about your parents. No matter how strict they are, they have your best interests at heart. They love you deeply. That's probably why they are so strict. Take the chance and tell them. You may be very surprised to see how they come through for you with flying colors. My own daughter recently asked me, "Mommy, what would you do if I came home and told you I was pregnant?" I thought about it a minute, asking myself what I would *really* do. "What do you think I would do?" I asked. "You would kill me," she said, "I mean you would really be angry." "I would be upset of course," I answered. "But what is done is done. I would take you for an immediate abortion," I said. "And then you would go straight to a convent." She laughed and so did I. Of course if she actually became pregnant we would take a lot of time to discuss options, and in reality I would not force her to have an abortion if she didn't want one, and I would not send her to a convent. I *would* take measures to insure that she not get pregnant again (give more lectures on being selective about sex, probably give in and help her to get birth control—

something I have so far been unwilling to do in the hope that my young daughter will choose to wait until she is more mature to have sex).

Anyway, what came of the conversation was the realization on my part how terrified of their parents teenage girls are when it comes to the subject of pregnancy. If my own daughter could say something like "You would kill me"—and I am known to be understanding and "sisterly"—how much more terror must be felt by other teens who have parents who are more strict (but no less loving) than I. Yet I have spoken about this subject with hundreds of mothers and fathers, ranging from ultra-liberal to super-strict, and each one has emphatically told me that he or she would stick by the child and help her to resolve the problem. They all admitted that they would be angry, but not one of them said they would be so angry as to reject or abandon a daughter in trouble. Furthermore, all of them hoped their child would trust them enough to confide in them. So, if you are pregnant, give it a long hard "think" and dare to confide in your parents. Perhaps here's where the old adage, "Blood is thicker than water," comes in. When real trouble comes, everything but love gets put aside and you can almost always count on your closest blood relatives—your parents.

If, however, you really feel you can't tell your parents about your pregnancy, for whatever reason, speak to your school counselor. She will respect your privacy and possibly arrange for an appointment with a family planning service in your neighborhood. In many cases total privacy is respected, and your decision will be kept from anyone other than those helping you. But this varies from community to community. So if you are determined not to let your parents find out, call in advance to inquire about whether the privacy of minors is guaranteed. You can also call the national number of Planned Parenthood (212-541-7800).

They will refer you to a local chapter near you. If you want to write instead, the address is: 810 Seventh Avenue, New York, NY 10019.

You may decide to have and keep your baby. If you do, you have a rough road ahead of you. I really don't think it's a good idea, either for your sake or the baby's. You will be giving up the years of freedom that you need to allow you to become a well-balanced adult, and your baby won't be getting the kind of mature mother who can take the best care of a baby. You may be lucky enough to have a parent who is willing to do most of the work of caring for the baby while you yourself are "growing up," but even so you must realize that the ultimate responsibility for that baby is yours. I don't say you should absolutely not choose to have and care for the baby. In your case it just may be the right choice. Only you can decide that. But right or wrong, it will certainly be a very difficult choice, and one whose immediate consequences—a child who needs you —will be with you for the rest of your life.

Let's not forget about the father of the child. If he's been a meaningful part of your life, he should play a role in any decision you reach on how to deal with the pregnancy. If he is a loving, caring person, and he wants to have the child, you'll want to take that into consideration. Although I think two teenagers trying to raise a child will face many difficulties, I don't think the challenge is impossible. I myself am the product of a teenage pregnancy (and glad to be here). Also, I know some fine young people who have counted the cost and have still chosen to have the child— and who have so far done a fine job (although they admit that they had to give up a lot—an awful lot—to do it).

However, no matter what the father of the child thinks, remember, *you* are the one who will have to bear the child, so you should, after taking all things into consideration, be the one to make the final decision.

If you can't or won't keep the baby or have an abortion,

you can choose to give it up for adoption. As Nadeen pointed out, it is painful to do this, but you will be able eventually to go on and live a happy life.

Being pregnant, unmarried, and a teenager may be the toughest thing you'll ever face in your life. Don't bear it alone. Find someone to help you through it. Then grit your teeth, plow through the fear, and do what you have to do to make the best of a bad situation. It is bad, but it's not impossible. The only bad situation for which there is no remedy is death.

Death and pregnancy aren't the only terrible situations you may have to face. What's amazing isn't how many problems there are in life—but how well people can rise above them.

– COPING WITH OTHER TRAGEDIES –

Sixteen-year-old Roger says,

When I got into a car accident my whole face was messed up. I lost all my front teeth and my nose was pushed upside my head. My lip was split open. After I got out of the hospital I wouldn't even look in the mirror because what I would see was a monster. I wanted to die.

Six months later Roger says,

I got a bridge with perfect front teeth. After three weeks my lip went back to size. Then I had plastic surgery on my nose, and after a few months it looked as good as before or better—I'm not sure which. Once in a while I think I'm not as good looking as I was, but I try not to dwell on that.

Life goes on. Things have a way of working themselves out—with a little help from you, your friends, and your family. People have overcome all sorts of tragedies. As mentioned before, Dwight D. Eisenhower suffered a knee injury that prevented him from becoming a professional football player. He couldn't play ball so he became president of the United States. Sometimes an accident is for the purpose of changing the direction of your life.

Others have suffered from blindness. Think of John Milton, the famous English poet who wrote *Paradise Lost*. His gradual blindness didn't stop him from writing some of the greatest works in English literature, works that are loved and enjoyed to this day. Ray Charles and Stevie Wonder are blind, yet they are among the most successful musicians who have ever lived.

Think of other famous people you know about who have survived—and even triumphed over—terrible disabilities. There are a lot of just ordinary people who have done the same. But, of course, then they're not ordinary. And neither are you. You'll be amazed by how much inner strength you can find once you look for it.

My own father, at the age of seventeen, lost a leg in a train accident, yet he became an amateur boxing champion—fighting with one artificial leg (from just below the knee).

A tragedy is one of the best ways to bring out your inner strength—your hidden store of power—your will to live and excel.

A tragedy can also make us grow spiritually. It is only after we have felt and gotten through great personal psychological and even physical pain that we can truly understand how other people feel when they suffer. Having gone through "hell" yourself, you will find yourself being compassionate (feeling for) others who suffer. You will be able to comfort someone else, to give that person the love and understanding needed. When you reach out and help another sufferer it will be as if you were going back and reaching out and helping yourself when you were suffering. You'll find a strange and wonderful joy when you give that help to someone who is in desperate need of it — someone who may not ever expect you to be so understanding.

Comforting others from personal experience makes you a deeper, more sensitive, more mature person. Indeed, you become what the Jewish expression terms a "mensch" or a "real person."

The only reason I can help teenagers today is because of the many personal tragedies I myself have suffered. Had I had an easy time of it, had my life been as the cliché goes, "a bed of roses," I would never be able to speak with understanding about real pain and ways to overcome it. People would detect my lack of deep feeling and would think "Easy for you to say."

So remember, the further down into the depths of your soul the tragedy reaches, the deeper, the more compassionate, the more loving the person you will be — especially if you deal with the problem the best way you can. It's not the short run that counts, but the long run.

Saying: *In the long run.*

12

Whatever Happened to God?

God has gotten himself a bad reputation! Some of you may have heard that God is watching you from the sky and making a record of every wrong thing you do. You figure that by now he must have quite a list against you. So you'd just as soon not meet him.

There are so many people speaking for God—telling you what you must believe about him "or else." Perhaps you've gotten to the point where the whole issue of God is so confusing you don't know what to think, so you don't think much about it at all.

The way I see it, God has to be greater than any holy book or religion invented to describe him. I suspect that he's a lot more sensitive, intelligent, and understanding than many well-meaning religious people ever imagined. Unfortunately, however, we tend to make God over in our own, flawed image—instead of accepting that we were made in his, perfect image.

– WHAT IS GOD REALLY LIKE? –

Let's start with the basics. God is a spirit or energy—the energy that keeps the basic material of the universe together. That's why he can be everywhere at the same time. But more than energy, God is a personality—an intelligence. He knows everything. But he's a loving personality—in fact, God *is* love.

Now, if such a God existed, would it be worth your while to get to know him?

– HOW KNOWING GOD CAN HELP YOU –

I don't care what you say. No one really understands you. God is the only one who really understands you.

Denise, 15.

If you know God you never feel completely alone. You always have someone to confide in—to talk to in your mind. It's like having a constant friend along, but a supremely wise and kind friend. After all, if God knows every thing, you can talk to him about anything and feel confident he will understand. Fourteen-year-old Jennifer believes:

You may not get an answer that minute, but you get an answer. It's just too close for comfort to believe it's a coincidence. It doesn't have to be that day—it depends on what the situation is—but it's, like, cleared up. In the end, I get the help I asked for.

Having faith in God makes you feel a lot better about the pressures in your life. It reassures you, as perhaps no human words can, that you will not be given pain or suffering in excess of what you can handle. Faith in God also gives you the sense of a presence whom you can turn to for comfort and help when you are suffering.

If you know God and you feel that he is always with you, you will not be so afraid any more—again because you will know that he would never let anything happen to you that wasn't ultimately going to turn out for the good. You might still be afraid at times, but you would never crack up.

God can also help you with guilt. If you believe in God, then you can turn to him when you have done something wrong and ask for help in setting things right again. People who have a simple faith in God often save themselves thousands of dollars in psychiatric fees—and many hours of torment. God is an immediate source of forgiveness.

Okay. So maybe it would be worth your while to check into this God idea. How do you do it?

– HOW TO FIND GOD –

All you have to do is talk to him in your mind. It doesn't matter where you do this. It can be walking in the street, lying in your bed late at night or in a place of worship.

What should you say? Talk to God naturally. Say what's on your mind. Since you probably doubt whether he's really there at all you might say something like:

God, if you're really there, I want to get to know you. I'm afraid in a way. Please help me.

I did that. I even asked God to give me a sign that he really existed and that he heard me calling for his help. Little bits and pieces began to come together for me and I found myself asking, "Was that you, God?" A strange-seeming coincidence here, a dream that answered a question there, the sudden appearance of a solution to a problem I had been worrying over for a long time—I began to wonder. Could this be true? Is there really a God? And is he talking to me?

You may not want to ask for a sign. You can perhaps find God by being in touch with God wherever you can find him. You may detect God in your own feelings of goodness and kindness, in all the beauties of the world, in nature, in the warmth and generosity of other people. If you look for him in the right places you will find him. You may not ever need to ask for a sign because you may begin to see signs of his goodness everywhere. You may find yourself talking to God all the time in the most natural way—thanking him for the wonderful life around you, calling upon the power of his goodness so that you can choose to do the right thing when put to the test.

If you talk to God all the time, just by your constant effort to communicate with him you will gradually come to know him. Don't wait for the time when you are in trouble —because, although God will surely not turn away from you simply because he's never heard from you before, you will find it easier to get through if you've already established lines of communication.

Once you have a little faith, once you become accustomed to talking to God and start to feel sure that he is listening to you, you are "praying." What most people mean by prayer is getting down on their knees, folding their hands together and asking for a lot of favors. That, too, is prayer. But the kind of praying I'm talking about can help you feel God's presence within you at all times, and that is the very essence of prayer—communion with God.

– PRAYER OR TALKING TO GOD ON A REGULAR BASIS –

I think the best conversations with God do not take place on bended knee but on foot. Somehow getting on your knees to pray seems too "official." And anyway, it's not always convenient to get down on your knees. It seems much easier just to talk to God as things come up. For example, if you're feeling depressed about a negative relationship you're in and you just don't know how to find the strength to break it off, why not turn your worries into a prayer?

> God, what am I going to do? This relationship is dragging me down. How am I going to get out of this? I've tried so many times and I just can't seem to end it.

When that thought is simply a worry, you tend to just repeat it over and over and get nowhere with it. When you turn it into a prayer, you tend to find an answer. Why is this so?

Some people say that prayer works only for psychological reasons. They argue that when you pray, you calm down, and by putting your worries into the form of a question, you open yourself to believing in the possibility of an answer. Once you believe in the possibility of an answer—of a way out of your trouble—you get one. You put your mind into the state of being willing to do the right thing. They argue, therefore, that both the answer and the strength come to you, not from any outside source, but from within yourself. In a way they're right. This is the way prayer works. Who says God has to be somewhere up in the sky? He can be, and he is, right there in your mind, too.

But then why pray? Why not just talk to yourself? Why?—because many people have trouble answering their own questions. Instead of solving their problems, they just continue to worry. My advice is: pray.

Above and beyond prayer, there is something else that shows the presence of God. It looks like simply coincidence, but its effects are miraculous. People have come to think of this phenomenon as "Amazing Grace."[1]

– AMAZING GRACE AND HOW IT WORKS –

Amazing Grace can be seen when you have a "close call," such as getting hit by a car and getting up and walking away without a scratch, or when your parents decide not to stay out late after all and return home to discover the house in flames and you unconscious upstairs. It is the thousands of narrow escapes from disaster that we experience in our own lives and read about in the newspaper. It's all those things that seem like an incredible stroke of luck. Some call it luck. But I call it grace, and it surely is amazing.

Twenty-three-year-old Gary tells how his life was saved:

After years of trying to become good enough to com-

---

[1]Scott M. Peck, M.D., *The Road Less Traveled* (Simon & Schuster, 1978). Dr. Peck discusses this phenomenon in detail in section IV of his book, entitled "Grace" (pp. 234–316).

pete with champion bodybuilders, I was so depressed that I found myself doing coke. First a little and then a lot, so much that I had to deal it to keep up my own supply. Soon I started shooting up heroin, too. I lost weight—looked like a wreck and hated myself for being a failure. One morning I decided, "This is it. I'm going to kill myself tonight." I went to work knowing that I was going to be fired that day (I had heard it through the grapevine) and sure enough, I was. I was getting my things together when I was told that someone was on the phone for me. It was a guy I knew from the gym—two years ago. He said, "Gary, are you all right? I don't know why, but you've been on my mind and all day I kept getting this strong feeling to call you." I told him, "No, as a matter of fact I'm not all right," and I spilled the whole story about the drugs. He said, point blank, "You have to make a decision right now. Do you want to live or die? If you want to live, you can. Your will can save you." I thought about it real hard and I knew I wanted to live. I said, "Yes." He told me I would have to go into a live-in drug program. This guy spent the whole day on the phone until he got me into a program. I was away for a month drying out and talking to psychologists. They also found out that I had a serious case of hepatitis. I would have died within three months if I had kept up the drugs. Now, 3 years later, I have a good job as a restaurant manager and I do modeling and health and fitness seminars on the side. Thinking back, were it not for that phone call, I would have killed myself for sure. I was at the end of the line. It makes me think—somebody up there is looking after me!

What kind of message got through to Gary's friend and made him call at the exact moment when Gary most needed help? Stories like this really help us to believe in the existence of a power for good in this world—which most of us call God. And there are so many such stories.

Talk to people and you'll find out that almost everyone has a story about how they narrowly escaped death or injury or some other disaster. Here's mine. One day I was driving along, daydreaming, and I turned into oncoming traffic. A truck hit my small car and sent it flying through the air. My car landed on a parked car which hit a parked motorcycle. My car, the truck that hit me, the car I hit, and the motorcycle were *all* totally destroyed. But I emerged (after crawling through the crushed window) without a scratch. The truck driver was unhurt, but he was protected by the size of his truck. Why was I, in a tiny Toyota, spared? Call it a coincidence, call it good luck, or maybe, call it "Amazing Grace."

Think of your own life. Were there times when life seemed to work for you—to save you from some potential disaster, when someone appeared to offer you help just when you desperately needed it, when some catastrophe that you *knew* was inevitable miraculously did not occur, for no reason you were ever able to figure out? What do you think about it now?

"Amazing Grace" can also operate in small ways, such as the arrival of an encouraging letter from out of the blue just when you're most depressed. It can be a phone call, a chance meeting, a song on the radio at just the right moment that turns your mood around and saves you from sinking into despair. All of this, I believe, is a part of "Amazing Grace." It is what I always think of when I hear the expression, "God works in mysterious ways, his wonders to perform."

– THE MIRACLE OF LIFE –

The mysterious and miraculous are not limited to human experience. They can be seen in creation itself. The evolution of all of nature as well as the human race from a one-celled amoeba—what intelligence is behind it all? Some people are against teaching evolution because they think it suggests that God doesn't exist. I think the very opposite. How wonderful that God set into motion this extraordinary process, and that we through our study of nature with the brains God gave us, can gain some understanding of the world he created.

How is it that a baby can be developed from a simple sperm and egg? Why is the genetic coding just right to produce the exact organs needed for human beings to function? How is it that the crocodile, the monkey, and the elephant, not to mention the whale and the giraffe, such strangely diverse creatures, can all survive and thrive on this planet? What keeps the tide from flooding the earth, the sun, moon and stars from falling from the sky, the temperature from rising so high or so low that we are destroyed? Scientists try to discover what God in his infinite wisdom ordained for our pleasure and our well-being. Some day, perhaps, they will be able to explain why the miracle of nature works so well. But they're a long way away from that now. They only know that it does.

Dr. Scott M. Peck, psychologist and author of the best-selling book *The Road Less Traveled*, says,

> To explain the miracles of grace and evolution we hypothesize the existence of a God who wants us to grow—a God who loves us. To many this hypothesis seems too simple, too easy; too much like a fantasy; childlike and naive. But what else do we have?. . . .
> No one who has observed the data and asked the

question has been able to produce a better hypothesis or really a hypothesis at all. Until someone does, we are stuck with this strangely childlike notion of a loving God or else with a theoretical vacuum.[2]

– GOD AS I KNOW HIM –

Now let me tell you about God as I know him. I think God has a great sense of humor. Why else would he have created the odd-looking elephant with its long trunk, the kangaroo who hops around with her babies in built-in pockets, and the toothy, leathery crocodile?

Next, he's brilliant. Otherwise how could he cause so many millions of things to come together in what we call "coincidence?" I think he likes to keep us guessing about him—and that's why he takes the time to do things in such a subtle way. It's how he gives us a chance to think for ourselves.

Another thing about God is, he's never shocked. No matter how horrific your deed, he's seen it before. Instead of being disgusted with you, he feels sorry for you. I imagine him looking down at us when we're condemning ourselves and wondering how we can ever forgive ourselves and saying, "Give yourself a break."

The God I know is also gentle. He doesn't force himself on anyone. He never butts into your life unless you ask him to. But he can read minds, so it doesn't matter if you ask him with words or not. If your heart is crying out for help, even if you have not addressed God directly, he will help you. That's how sensitive he is. I believe that many people (maybe you) have been praying to him without even realizing it—and that he's been answering them, too,

[2]Ibid. p. 269

again without their even knowing it was he who answered. (Who knows, maybe your reading this book is one of his ways of answering you?)

But God never imposes his will on you. Instead of trying to run your life according to his will, he limits his intrusion into your life according to your own will. You decide how much of God you want.

Another thing about God. I think he likes to see you have a good time. I think he loves to see you laughing and joking and enjoying life. He gets a kick out of it when you're out there playing in the nature he created—baking in the sun, leaping over the ocean waves at the beach, hiking through the thick forests and gazing at the full moon and bright stars.

Maybe the best thing I love about God is the way he accepts everyone. He doesn't care what anyone looks like, dresses like or acts like. If you want to deal with him, you're okay with him. A few years ago, when Appolonia accepted Prince's People's Award, she shocked everyone by looking up and with tears in her eyes saying, "Thank you, God, because without you, none of this would have happened." There was a dead hush in the audience as Appolonia with her dress cut down to here and up to there, made her way back to her place. The next day some comments were made: "Hmmph, I'm surprised to hear *her* talking about God. She doesn't look very religious." But I don't think God cares one little bit how "religious" or "non-religious" you are. I just think it fills him with great joy when you invite him into your life and when you remember to thank him for his presence and his help.

The God I know wants you to be filled with joy, too. That's why he's made it so easy for you to find that feeling. All you have to do is do something good—for yourself or for someone else—and you get that strange feeling inside, like you're walking on air or even flying. You feel powerful—wonderful—above it all. God gives better highs than any chemical substance can possibly produce.

I'm not afraid of God any more. I used to be afraid of him when I was a teenager because I didn't know him at all—I only knew "about him"; but what I knew about him was all wrong. I had been listening to people who didn't really know him themselves. Lucky for me, over the years, I got to know him firsthand.

Firsthand. That's the only way anyone can really get to know God. That's why if you're interested in finding out more about God you'll have to go to the source—you'll have to start talking to him in your mind. Instead of asking everyone else questions about him, why don't you ask him? You may be surprised at the answers you receive.

Saying: *Amazing Grace.*

13

Famous Cop-Outs: Breaking the Habit

Everyone is looking for a quick fix. Hey, who ever said you're not supposed to feel any pain? "Oh, I smoked pot because my brother was killed." Did your brother come back from the grave since you smoked pot?

David Toma

If you've ever gotten high, by now you know that the big problem with getting high is that the pain you were trying to escape is still there when you come down. Getting high does nothing to change a bad situation (except sometimes to make it worse).

Why is it so wrong to get high anyway? I used to wonder what would happen if someone discovered a way to get high that was cheap, legal, and would produce no damaging physical effects. If such a discovery were made, would getting high still be wrong?

It would destroy the human race. Think about it for a moment. What if something as harmless and as inexpensive as water were there for you to use whenever you wanted to—to get you stoned out of your mind. What would you do?

If you're anything like most people, the moment you had a slight problem or were momentarily bored you'd reach for a quick dose and find immediate escape. Why not?

No one would be straight. Your teachers would be flying high—teaching nonsense to a stoned class who could care less. Your bus drivers would be whacked out, crashing into drivers who were also blitzed out of their minds. People in government, those who run the business world, the medical profession—everyone would be flying high. Who would be able to resist the temptation? When you think about it, isn't it only when they start to discover the harmful effects of a drug that people start to give it up? (See bibliography for books detailing various forms of drugs and alcohol.)

So you see, it's a good thing we can't get high all the time. It would be too tempting. The way I see it, the only high that's a good high is one that comes from within—the kind you get when you accomplish something great and you feel as if you're on top of the world, or when you do something good for someone else and you get that "light" feeling.

The trouble is, we don't want to wait for these natural highs. We're impatient. It takes a long time to accomplish something, and can be a lot of work to help people. We want an instant high—we want the high without paying the price of the work. But there's no such thing as a free ride. You can buy the instant high, but the price you pay is a lot more than the money you spend. You pay with your self-respect. The fact is, had you waited for the natural high that comes when you achieve something or help someone, your self-respect would be increased permanently—with no bad side effects.

Getting high is not the only way to escape problems in the wrong way. Aside from using cocaine, heroin, acid, pot, and alcohol, we smoke cigarettes, sleep around, spend hours in front of the boob tube, overeat, and shoplift, —all in a desperate attempt to escape reality. Soon what seemed like a pleasurable escape becomes a dreary, numbing, depressing, and self-destructive habit from which we get little or no pleasure. But it's become a habit and now we can't escape the escape.

– DRUGS –

In order to break a negative habit, you have to first believe that the habit is harming you—draining your energy and stealing your time.

Let's start with drugs. You probably know all about what can happen on drugs. Drugs steal your freedom. You become a slave, a beggar, a victim—of cocaine or crack, for example. You find yourself doing anything just to get some. You lose control of yourself and you start to despise yourself. Sixteen-year-old David says,

> Do you know how many girls I've seen go with a guy (I mean to bed) just to get that crack? If it wasn't for crack guys could never get those girls.

Fifteen-year-old Tammy says,

I would do anything as long as I could be high doing it. Sometimes I'd steal from my father's wallet when he was sleeping. One day I pretended the house was robbed. I took all the cash that my father brought home from his business. My parents found out. That's when they put me in this drug rehabilitation program upstate. Now I've been off drugs for almost four months. I never want to be like I was. I don't know what would have happened to me if my parents hadn't put me in that program.

Seventeen-year-old Danny says,

When I snort that first line I feel superior-happy, strong.

But what happens the next day?

I'm always so embarrassed to see the people I was with because I usually said so many stupid things—like I was telling this guy I didn't even know that I admire him and stuff. When I think of it I don't even want to see any of those people again. But the worst part is I always get so depressed the day after I do coke. And if I can't get any more I'll try some booze —whatever I can get.

What is the price of a two minute or a two hour high?—sometimes a two day depression. You also pay with the gradual deterioration of your mind and your body. Try to concentrate on a difficult math problem the day after doing a lot of coke. Try to run five miles and then lift weights in the gym for two hours. Your mind will not be able to focus on the problem and your body will scream at you: "Leave me alone." Every muscle fiber will feel as if it is being ripped apart.

You may think you're getting away with it because you recover after a day or two, but keep it up and one day "boom"—it will hit you. No more fast recoveries. You can't think straight and you're always getting sick. You could even die. Coke and crack are really long term downers, after a very brief up.

What about marijuana, or "weed"? A whole generation grew up believing it was harmless, but those people, who are now in their late twenties and early thirties, are not smoking any more. Why?

Twenty-seven-year-old Laurina says,

> I stopped smoking pot about two years ago. I did it because so many of my friends had stopped and they kept telling me that pot was the reason my life was at a standstill. I was in a boring job where the manager was not as intelligent as I was, but I kept telling myself it didn't matter. That's the way life is. After I quit smoking pot—about three or four months I think—I got this bright idea to answer some want ads just to see if I could get a better job. I took a day off from work, and in one day I got three job offers. I took the one that offered me double my salary, a car and an expense account. I'm selling computer equipment and I love it. Now I see how pot was making me lazy. But then I couldn't see it. I thought people were just being fanatics when they said pot affects your brain. Now I try to tell people who still smoke, and it's hard to convince them. If they would stop for good they'd see a big difference.

Keep smoking pot. You'll never know what you missed —what you could have done, what you could have been.

Studies have been done to prove that engineering students who smoked pot for two years could no longer do mathematical problems they solved simply two years before. The proof is in. Pot does destroy brain cells. That's why everyone is stopping. Guess what. It's no longer cool to smoke dope. It's getting to the point where if you smoke pot you're considered a loser.

– CIGARETTES –

True, cigarettes won't ruin your life by rotting your brain or stealing your motivation, but they can take your life with lung cancer, cancer of the larynx, emphysema, or heart failure, so we'd better talk about them.

Why do people smoke? Did you know that you get a mild high each time you have a cigarette? When you smoke, the nicotine causes your liver to convert stored animal fat to sugar which is released into your bloodstream. This shot of sugar to your bloodstream gives you a physical lift—similar to what you feel just after eating a candy bar. The inhalation of the smoke also deadens your nerve endings, giving you a calm, pleasant feeling.

But just like any other high, the cigarette high eventually lets you down—lower than when you started. "When the extra shot of sugar gives you the pleasant high, it also triggers a squirt of insulin from the pancreas, lowering the blood sugar level and bringing a gradual feeling of fatigue or tension. The fatigue or tension leads to the desire for the high of another cigarette to overcome the bad feeling."[1]

Looks like there really are no free rides. You pay a price even for the mild high of a simple cigarette. You become addicted. The nicotine in cigarettes is one of the most addictive substances of all. That's why it's so incredibly hard to quit smoking. You lose your freedom. If that were not so, why would millions of people rather die of lung cancer and other deadly diseases than give up smoking?

[1]James H. Hoke, *I Would If I Could and I Can* (New York: Berkley Books, 1980), p. 157.

Most people who smoke started when they were teenagers. They all hated the taste of the cigarette at first, and they all choked on the first few drags, but determined to prove that they could do it, they persisted. Maybe that's you. Okay. So you proved something you had to prove at that time. Now it's time to give it up. It may seem to you as if you've been smoking forever, but it's only a few years compared to the twenty or thirty years of damage you'll have done by the time you're in your forties. If you can't stop smoking on your own, don't take that as a weakness. Get help. Ask your family doctor to refer you to a local stop-smoking program. There's one in every town.

Smokers remind me of a bunch of babies looking for something to suck on—something to replace the old bottle or pacifier. Could it be that a false sense of security is found in dragging on a cigarette? You don't carry your "blankie" around any more. You gave up your pacifier a long time ago. Don't grow into a thirty-year-old adult with a smoky pacifier. Reject smoking now, while you're still young.

– INDISCRIMINATE SEX –

Sex, for the right reason, at the right time, is one of the best things that can ever happen to you. But sex with someone you don't care about, as an escape from loneliness or depression, can only lead to more loneliness and depression, because once the sex act is over, you feel empty.

The incredible intimacy of the sex act tells you there should be a loving, caring, understanding connection between you and your sex partner. When there isn't, you feel lonlier than ever, and may be driven to look for someone else to relieve *that* loneliness. Before you know it, you're having sex with lots of different partners. And you keep feeling worse and worse. Not only are you lonely, but you lose more of your self-respect each time you go looking for love in a place you will never find it.

Sexual promiscuity these days is a lot more than a threat to your psychological well-being. You can get all sorts of diseases, some of which don't show up until years later. These diseases—venereal diseases, herpes, AIDS—can cause everything from infertility to death itself.

It should be clear to you that sex is the wrong way to escape the depression of loneliness. If you have been promiscuous in the past, however, don't make the mistake of thinking that you are "ruined" and that there's no way out. There's always a way back to self-respect, if you only look for it.

– EXCESSIVE TELEVISION VIEWING –

Television and movies are perhaps among the least harmful cop-outs—or are they? Living in a world of make-believe, getting your experiences through other people, can rob you of your own real life. Did anyone ever come out of that television screen and ask you to join the chase? Were you given money recently through the television?

If you've been watching more than 10 hours of television a week, you're probably using television to escape from life. This kind of excessive television viewing clutters your subconscious mind with junk. It hinders creative thinking. Instead of being free to work on ways to make your life better, your subconscious mind is jammed with confusing and irrelevant images. A good way to tell if this is happening to you is by your dreams. Are they filled with bits and pieces of television shows you've watched?

Don't take your mind for granted. Instead of filling it with anything that flashes across the screen, exercise quality control over what goes into it. Instead of falling asleep to the drone of television voices, put on relaxing music or self-help tapes. Today you can find cassettes of almost anything: beautiful poetry, novels, jokes, and even the Bible. Think how much more pleasant your dreams will be.

– EXCESSIVE EATING –

Some people get into the bad habit of eating when they're bored, depressed, or lonely. Nobody loves them so they eat with two forks. Without realizing it, most of these people are trying to fill any empty space with something that cannot fill it. Food cannot take the place of missing love. It can't make you permanently secure, either. The food going into your stomach makes you feel temporarily soothed. But when you've stuffed yourself you feel more depressed than ever. When you start to look fat you become even more depressed.

– STEALING –

Why do people steal? While it is true that some people steal because they are starving and must survive, most people steal for other reasons. They steal because they are angry. Something is missing in their lives and they want to get even with life for robbing them—so they rob in turn. "I'll even up the score," they say, deep down in their subconscious minds. "I have this coming to me."

If you do a lot of stealing, maybe you're trying to get

revenge on life for having treated you badly. Your parents don't understand you and you're frustrated, so you steal. You hate your father because he's always picking on you, so you steal. Your parents favor your older brother, so you steal.

The trouble with stealing is that you just can't even up the score that way. In fact, you make things worse because every time you steal you lose self-respect. Deep down inside you despise yourself.

– HOW TO BREAK THE HABIT— ANY HABIT –

The only way to break a habit is to use your mind. Your mind consists of two parts: the conscious mind (the part that listens to all the facts and makes logical decisions), and the subconscious mind (the part that digests all the information supplied by the conscious mind and comes up with creative solutions). In order to break a habit your conscious (logical) mind must think of all the reasons to break that habit.

Think about how that habit is hurting you. If it's drugs, picture how the drugs are eating up your brain cells. If it's cigarettes, think of how your lungs are getting blacker each time you smoke. And so forth.

Next, think about how much you want to be healthy again. Picture how good it will be to think clearly and be intelligent. Imagine how your lungs will improve and how you'll be able to run or swim without getting out of breath.

Then motivate yourself by picturing how stupid you look when you engage in the habit. If it's cocaine, picture your desperate expression as you sniff the white powder eagerly, secretively. Picture yourself jabbering away like an idiot. If it's cigarettes, imagine how you look desperately sucking away at that adult pacifier. If it's stealing, picture yourself looking furtively around before you conceal the item in your jacket or purse—how you skulk around the store afterwards worrying if the security guard has seen you. Say to yourself, "I don't want to look this way any more."

Now picture other people you have seen engaging in the habit. How ridiculous they look. Think of how pathetic the guy who brags about his sexual conquests is—how his anxious face tells of his unhappiness even while he's talking about how great it was. Think of how disgusting your friend looked when he got drunk—what a fool he made of himself. Say to yourself, "I don't want to be like that."

Now bring back all the negative experiences you had as a result of this bad habit. Remember the time you threw up in your bed after drinking all night. Recall the disgusting feeling you got when you ate everything in the refrigerator. Remember the headache you had the time you did coke and drank Jack Daniel's all night. Say to yourself, "I reject this habit. I hate the way it makes me feel."

Now that your conscious mind has a list of good reasons to break the habit, your subconscious mind is ready to go to work.

You can use imagination to condition your subconscious mind to reject the bad habit. Picture yourself thinking about your bad habit as you read this description. Replace alcohol in your mind with whatever your problem is.

Imagine yourself thinking about your favorite alcoholic beverage. You can clearly visualize the beverage. You know you would like to decrease your use of alcohol because of the problems it creates for you and those around you.

You direct your mind to give you control over

your drinking. You picture a switch in your mind that controls your desire for alcohol. When the switch is turned off, you lose your taste for alcohol.

Now you can see your alcoholic drink even more clearly, but you're amazed to find that you have lost your taste for the drink. In fact, you see that you have lost all interest in alcohol, and you develop a great satisfaction in your ability to control your desire for drinking. You begin to think of other drinks that are nonalcoholic, and you begin to develop a taste for them.

You see yourself in a party situation where a drink is being offered to you, and you picture yourself turning it down. . . . You remember all of the bad sensations and feelings that alcohol always gives you, especially the day after you drink.

These memories become extremely vivid whenever an opportunity for drinking alcohol comes up.[2]

By playing a similar picture game in their minds, people have cured themselves of cancer. (They picture the body's immune system of white cells eating up the cancerous cells.) You can use picturing (or, as it's often called, imaging, or creative visualization) to reject bad habits. It really works. People have stopped smoking, given up drugs and alcohol, stopped overeating, and become free of many other habits by using this method. The mental "switch" is especially effective. In your mind, turn the switch which controls the desire for this thing to "off." Tell yourself the desire is "off." It cannot come back unless you turn it "on."

The method works because it is based upon your will, which is the most powerful force you have. It is your will

[2]Donald L. Wilson, M.D., *Total Mind Power* (New York: Berkley Books, 1979), pp. 171–75.

that turns the switch off and it is only your will that can turn it on. Remember that. Once you truly understand it, you will never again be the victim of a bad habit.

But what if you can't seem to mobilize your will to break the habit? Suppose you've tried to use all the self-help methods and they just didn't work. You feel hopelessly hooked. Take courage. Your will can still do the job. But it may need professional, outside help to show it the way.

Today, fortunately, there are many agencies set up with the express purpose of helping people to break free of alcohol and drug addiction. These agencies were set up because there are millions of teenagers who have become physically and psychologically addicted to substances (alcohol or drugs) that they can no longer say no to. In cases like that, the most courageous thing you can do is to make a phone call—to ask for help. The call itself is an act of will. You are saying, "I want to live. I want to be free." There is nothing weak or shameful about asking for help.

Here are some national organizations you can call if you are in need of help. If you call them, they will tell you the location of the nearest local branch so that you can contact that branch and begin to get immediate help.

Alcohol Problems

1. *Al-Anon Family Group Headquarters*
   P.O. Box 182
   Madison Square Station
   New York, NY 10017 (212) 481-6565

2. *Alcoholics Anonymous*, General Services
   468 Park Avenue S.
   New York, NY 10016 (212) 686-1100

3. *International Halfway House Association*
   500 N. Washington
   Alexandria, VA 22314 (703) 549-7202

4. *National Listen American Club*
   7545 Jurupa Avenue
   Riverside, CA 92504 (714) 688-2301

5. *Synanon Church*
   P.O. Box 786
   6055 Marshall-Petaluma Rd.
   Marshall, CA 94940 (415) 663-8111

Drug Abuse Problems

1. *National Family Council Against Drug Abuse*
   40 Westminster Drive
   Pearl River, NY 10965 (914) 735-9250

2. *Odyssey Institute*
   656 Avenue of the Americas
   New York, NY 10010 (212) 691-8510

3. *Pil-Anon Family Program*
   120 Gracie Square Station
   New York, NY 10028 (212) 744-2020

4. *Pills Anonymous*
   P.O. Box 473, Ansonia Station
   New York, NY 10023 (212) 874-0700

5. *Potsmokers Anonymous*
   316 E. Third Street
   New York, NY 10009 (212) 254-1777

6. The Coke Hotline: (800) 262-2463

This last number works for every state on the continen-
tal United States. If the number is busy, call your local
telephone information number and ask for the drug hotline
in your town. Today virtually every town, no matter how
small, has such a number.

Whether you are able to kick the habit that has been holding you back by yourself, or whether you kick the habit with the assistance of professionals, consider yourself a real winner for having the courage to get angry enough to do something about the negative force that has taken control of your life.

Saying: *Break the habit before it breaks you!*

14

Before You Pull the Trigger, Make the Leap, Swallow the Pills, Drink the Hemlock... Think of This

---

My heart aches, and a drowsy numbness pains
    My sense, as though of hemlock I had drunk,
Or emptied some dull opiate to the drains
    One minute past, and Lethe-wards had sunk.[1] ...

                                        John Keats

You think that nobody understands the horrible way you feel. You can't believe that this state is ever going to end and you are sure that suicide is the only way out. Death seems a welcome relief from it all, and like the Romantic poet John Keats, you dream about slipping off into painless eternity.

[1] These are the first four lines of the poem "Ode to a Nightingale." It is included in *The Portable Romantic Reader*, Howard E. Hugo, ed. (New York: Viking press, 1957, p. 135) under the section entitled "Romantic Suicide."

Don't do it! In the words of Chuck Yaeger,

Life is as unpredictable as flying in combat.[2]

- JUST ONE MINUTE MORE -

Your entire life can change in a split second. You may quit just at the moment when your life was about to turn around—only you'll never know.

I remember an old cowboy movie I once saw. A man was traveling through the Sierra Nevada desert, and his horse died. As he walked for miles and miles his food and water ran out. Half-dead, he spied what he thought was a lake. Diving into it with glee, he discovered to his horror that he had seen a mirage—only his imagination playing tricks on him. So, discouraged by this false vision, he lay down to die in the hot sun. As the sun baked the last bit of life out of his body, the camera zoomed in on a scene twenty yards from where the man lay. Three gold miners were eating and drinking heartily in an old cabin. Just one more minute. Had the man held out for one more minute he would have been saved, but he let his discouragement get the best of him.

It's been my experience that when things look the worst, that's when they're sure to improve—if you dare to tough it out a little bit longer. It's what's known as bottoming out, or hitting bottom. Once you've done that, there's no place to go but up—if you're still around to go anywhere. Here's what happened to Phil, who is now twenty-two.

When I was eighteen I thought my life was over. I had lost my job and my girl, and my parents were threatening to kick me out. I thought about driving

[2]Chuck Yaeger and Leo Janis, *Yaeger* (New York: Bantam Books Inc., 1985). p. 330.

my car over the side of a bridge. I was thinking about doing it that afternoon, but then I decided to wait. I would go out that night and get drunk for the last time. That night I went to a bar where I met a woman who changed my entire life. She started talking to me and making sense. We became close friends. She helped me to get into business college and she got me reading all kinds of books. Soon my entire life started to turn around. Now I drive a Corvette, own my own auto repair shop, and have a few girls I see. If I had killed myself that afternoon what a fool I would have been. I never would have known what it feels like to be a success. One thing I know now. No matter how bad it is, don't give up. Something will happen! Every dog has its day!

You never know what can happen to turn things around for you. You could be reading a magazine, watching a television show, or sitting in your English class, when suddenly an idea will be presented to you that will change your entire life. You can have a dream that will show you a new way to look at things. You could get into a minor car accident and meet the person you will eventually marry. You could turn a corner as you're walking to school and run smack into the one person you need to put your life on the right track. As psychologist Dr. Ernest Fitzgerald says,

> We can never say we are losers. We just don't know when or where the victory will come.[3]

Your life might not change in an instant, but you can bet on one thing: it will change. Nothing stays the same. The nature of life itself is change. When things are good, they don't stay that way forever, do they? Then why should things stay the same forever when they are bad? In the

[3]Dr. Ernest Fitzgerald, *How to Be a Successful Failure* (New York: Atheneum/SMI, 1978), p. 127.

words of the unknown philosopher: HANG IN THERE.

Fifteen-year-old Jonathan tells this story.

I used to live far away from school, and I would keep losing my transportation passes. At the time my father would get very upset (I never got along with him) and yell and scream at me and call me names. At times I would sit in the shower and cry, thinking, "Why don't I just die," and "Maybe I should kill myself"—all because of my bus and train pass. Now I look back and I think, "What was the big deal?" But then it was the end of the world.

Fourteen-year-old Audrey says,

I hated my mother so much, I thought, "I'll kill myself to hurt her." When people would tell me, "things will get better," I used to think, "It's easy for you to say because you're sitting on the other side." One day I went in the bathroom and cut my wrists, but I didn't die. After that I still didn't get along with my mother, but other things got better. If I had killed myself I would have been hurting myself more than my mother. I would have lost the only life I have just to get even with her—and after she cried and all, she would still be alive, but I'd be dead.

Dr. Robert Schuller quotes a woman who nearly killed herself and was saved seconds before dying:

Everything that has happened since has been better than I could ever have dreamed. I wish I could tell everyone who's depressed, or anyone who's thought about dying or killing themselves that it passes: It may not seem like it but it does pass and it always gets better.[4]

[4]Dr. Robert Schuller, *The Be Happy Attitudes* (Texas: Word Book Publishers, 1985), p. 48.

Just one more hurdle to jump—then it will be easy riding for a while. We all go through what are called "passages." There are times when life gets tough. These hard times are like tests we have to pass in order to get to the next happy stage.

It was tough leaving your mother's womb. The first thing you did was cry. But then you became a contented baby. It was no joy giving up being a toddler. You didn't like having to sit in a classroom for hours—no more play all day long. It is tough making the transition from child to teenager. Suddenly you have to worry about being attractive to the opposite sex, how to convince your parents that you have a mind of your own, how to figure out what you want to do with the rest of your life. It will also be difficult making the transition from teenager to adult, but between —and even during—the changes are happy times.

If nothing else, you've got time on your side. Time will see to it (if you don't stop time by killing yourself) that you get older and become your own boss. Time will see to it that the pendulum swings back. So, if you are miserable now, you are sure to be happy later.

– MAKE BELIEVE YOU DID IT –

If you really feel tempted to kill yourself, try this idea first. Picture that you did it—you killed yourself. Imagine that you're dead. How does it feel to be completely gone —no more life at all? It feels so awful that, in fact, it's the one area that even your subconscious resists; people rarely if ever dream of their own deaths. If you're dreaming, you wake up. If you're imagining it realistically and vividly, as soon as you see yourself dead you'll wish you had a second chance. Your mind will calm down when you realize that you do—and that you want to give life a second chance, too. After all, death is *always* an option. But once you're dead, life can never be an option again. So what possible harm can there be in hanging around long enough to see if things do change for the better? Take an "I've got nothing to lose" attitude—because you don't.

– DON'T WALK OUT BEFORE THE GOOD PART –

What a shame it would be to walk out of the movie of your life right at the beginning. You'll be leaving before the plot of your life has had a chance to develop. You'll be walking out when the main character (you) is still having a hard time—before you ever get to the happy ending. You'll never find out what could have been.

I asked several adults who had had horrible teenage years to give some advice to other teenagers who are struggling.

Thirty-two-year-old Don, who is now a successful photographer earning over $200,000 a year, says,

I know you can't see it now, but if you hang in there you can eventually get everything you dreamed of. It just takes time.

Twenty-nine-year-old Dorothy, who owns a beauty shop, says,

When I think of how easy it is to kill yourself it scares me. If you do it you'll never know why you suffered so much as a teenager. I believe the more you suffer when you're younger, the better your life is later. At least that's true for me.

Twenty-five-year-old Vinnie, who's the lead singer in a band, says,

Killing yourself is the greatest act of weakness you can perform. Anyone can run away—that's easy. But if you stick it out your life will end up great. You have to pay your dues before you're sitting pretty.

What would have happened if Albert Einstein, who was a reject and a weirdo, had given in to depression and committed suicide? What if Walt Disney, who was so poor that he had to sleep in a cellar, had killed himself in despair? What if Ronald Reagan, as a teenager struggling to get into movies, had killed himself because he was depressed? He never would have become a movie star, much less governor of California and president of the United States.

Almost every teenager thinks of committing suicide. It's normal. Life seems unbearable and you get furious. You say, "I don't have to take this. I'll leave. I quit." But then you think better of it. You realize that there are other ways to get the pressure off your back. (Read the rest of this book to find out what they are—if you haven't done so already. And see the bibliography for books on teenagers who thought of or attempted suicide.)

– NO ONE CAN REPLACE *YOU* –

There is only one you. No one else can do what you were born to do. If you cut yourself off before your time you create a gap in the fabric of the universe—the life cycle. You break Karma. You commit a crime against nature itself. That's why a million alarm bells go off in your mind when you have that knife, gun, pill, or poison in your hand. Everything cries out: "No. No. Don't do this." The air itself is thick with a heavy feeling. Your heart beats a thousand times a minute. "No. No. No. Stop. Don't." You feel the resistance. You have to cut through a powerful force in order to kill yourself. You know it's wrong!

I thought of committing suicide when I was eighteen. I hated my physical appearance—I was bony and underdeveloped. I felt that my parents didn't understand me, and I felt isolated—cut-off. I had no real friends and no idea what to do with the rest of my life—what to become. I felt unworthy to live—every bad thing I had ever done flashed before my mind. I looked out the window of my sixth floor apartment in Queens, New York. I was going to jump to my death. I pictured myself falling. I imagined my head hitting the concrete and splitting open. I pictured my parents looking for me—calling my name. I wondered how long it would be before they noticed I was gone. I wondered if they would think to look out the window or would simply imagine that I had somehow slipped past them, where they sat in the living room, and gone out? Then I thought of death—how final it was. Next I worried about God. What if there was a hell . . . ?

I didn't jump. I know now that all of the pain I felt is what makes me able to talk to others who are in despair. My life has turned to be an exciting adventure. What a horror it would have been, what a loss for me (and, I like to think, for others), had I killed myself at eighteen. I would never have gotten to see how the plot of my life developed, would never have gotten to turn all the happy, successful corners that lead to where I am today.

– SET A CUT-OFF DATE –

So think about the fact that so many people are telling you that life does get better. Often the teenage years, which are billed as the happiest, are the very unhappiest. If you can just get through *them*, life will be a cinch. Try talking yourself into waiting until a certain age, at least. Say to yourself, "Okay. They say it gets better once you're an adult. If things don't improve by the time I'm 25, I'll kill myself." Interestingly enough, the suicide rate for teenagers is more than triple that of people in their late twenties and older. Could it be that things really do change—that there's something that you don't know that happens once you get out of your teens?

– REACH OUT FOR HELP –

Finally, before you pull the trigger, make the leap, swallow the pill . . . reach out to someone for help. Talk to anyone you trust. It can be a friend, a relative, a teacher, the parent of a friend, or even the local store clerk. Just blurt out your feelings.

If you can't do that, call your local suicide hotline. Call information to get the number of the suicide hotline in your city. There is one in every state and the telephone operators are sensitive to calls for such information. If you don't have the presence of mind to bother with information, *call the police*. They will get you the number, or at least talk to you.

Another good place to seek help is a local church or synagogue. Even if you do not practice the religion of that place of worship, you can be sure that they will help you. Every religion is established to help other people who are suffering. They are there for the express purpose of helping you. You won't be "bothering" them, but you will be giving them the chance to do the job they feel called to do. If anything you will give them joy because their goal is to be useful to people who suffer.

If you're still bound and determined to kill yourself, before you do it at least try this. Clear your mind and pray this prayer.

– THE EMERGENCY PRAYER –

Dear God:
    I see no reason to live. You're my last hope. Do something to save me. Amen.

As you pray, picture your words going straight up to God and see God listening to your prayer.

If you pray that prayer and mean it, I believe that something will happen to help you to change your mind; but it takes faith to pray that prayer. After all, you don't know whether there is a God in the first place, and if there is, whether he's listening to you or cares whether you live or die. But what have you got to lose? Even if it sounds silly to you, please try it. If you don't, you can't say for sure that it doesn't work, can you? Use this prayer whenever you're really desperate. I don't pretend to know why it always seems to work, but it does.

Choose life and you will live, maybe not happily ever after, but much more happily than you can ever imagine when you've hit a temporary low.

– REMEMBER THIS –

When the dark shadows come and tempt you to give up, remember:

> The woods are lovely, dark and deep
> But I have promises to keep,
> And miles to go before I sleep,
> And miles to go before I sleep.[5]

You have promises to keep, promises you've made to yourself and to others. It's not time for you to die. You have too much to accomplish first—miles to go before you sleep. Say to yourself, "Yes. It is tempting to die. These woods *are* lovely, dark and deep. But cold, too. I can't die yet. I have promises to keep. And miles—and years—before I sleep."

Saying: *I have promises to keep.*

[5]This is the last stanza of Robert Frost's poem, "Stopping by Woods on a Snowy Evening."

15

Friends in Trouble: How You Can Help

My friend's parents are really old-fashioned. They keep her locked up like a hermit. No trust. She told me she wants to kill herself. Now I can't sleep nights worrying about her. I wish I could do something. It's so scary.

Yvette, 14

It is scary when a friend is threatening to commit suicide, but there *is* something you can do about it.

Yvette is right to be concerned. Her friend is not just talking. Eight out of ten people who kill themselves talked about it to others before they did it. But on the up side, psychologists believe that the fact that the person is talking about it indicates that he or she is crying out for help— begging to be saved from that self-destructive act. You must try to answer that cry for help. Very often, people who are suicidal are not seriously mentally disturbed, and a warm, caring friend just like you can help save that person.

You might be thinking, "What's the use? People who threaten to kill themselves will do it sooner or later." Wrong. It has been established by psychologists that people who go through difficult periods in their lives and threaten or attempt suicide very often forget about the idea of suicide forever—once they get through that gloomy period.

What can you do? Most important of all, let your friend talk about it.

– LISTEN TO YOUR FRIEND –

Sometimes people are reluctant to let someone talk about suicide. They're afraid that once it is discussed, the idea becomes more real and may result in action—as though talking about it could make it happen. The exact opposite is in fact true. Talking about suicide gives the depressed person relief and enables him or her to put it off for a while—or forever.

Let your friend tell you all about what's bothering him or her. Ask lots of questions. Listen with empathy. Make supportive comments, such as: "I see what you mean," "Oh no," "He did that to you?" "No wonder you feel that way, anyone would," etc. Don't interrupt. Whatever you do, don't start saying things like, "You shouldn't feel that way," or "You're just mixed up." Never try to make light of his or her feelings, either because you think that will cheer him or her up or because you're uncomfortable dealing with such serious problems. Such comments only make your friend feel more alone and misunderstood. You want to make your friend feel that at least one person understands. The only way you can do this is by tuning in to your friend's feelings and taking them seriously—whether you think they are justified by the situation or not. This will be difficult because you may see clearly that your friend is all wrong in his or her thinking. Fifteen-year-old Karen made this mistake.

One day my friend called me and she was crying because her mother was yelling at her for failing in school and she wouldn't let her hang out with her friends any more. She said she was a failure and that she was going to take an overdose of pills. I said, "The only reason your mother yells at you is because she loves you and she wants you to succeed." She said, "If she loves me then why does she make me feel like a failure?"

But then Karen did the right thing:

Then I started to cry, and I said: "I need you. You are my best friend. Who will I go to for advice?" Then we talked some more and she said, "If it wasn't for you I would have killed myself."

As Karen discovered for herself, what a friend needs when everything looks bleak is the feeling of being loved and needed, not an argument justifying the bad things that have happened or the hurtful things others have done to him or her. Even though Karen was correct in what she said to the girl about her mother, that wasn't what her friend needed to hear then. It only made her feel more frustrated and angry than ever. It wasn't until Karen said, in effect, "I love you, I need you," that her friend calmed down and decided to live. Crying, in fact, might have been the best thing Karen could have done, because it let her friend know how deeply she felt about her. You may not be able to change the way other people treat your friend, but you do have the power to give your friend love.

People who are thinking of suicide have lost the ability to see any good in themselves or in life itself. You can try to find some for them.

– HELPING YOUR FRIEND TO FIND HOPE –

Following are several tactics to try. You'll have to be the judge of which might work on your friend. Start up a conversation that leads into: "What's the toughest thing you ever had to face?" You can give an example from your own life. Say something like: "For me it was the time I decided to go back home after I had run away. . . ." The main thing is just to get your friend to remember other tough things he or she has successfully faced before. You don't have to say much. You can express admiration for some particularly courageous act, but leave it at that. Whatever you do, resist the temptation to start preaching. Don't start saying things like, "See. You faced that situation, you can face this one, too." The idea is to let your friend come to that conclusion independently. That way it sticks. Your friend's self-esteem and self-confidence rise, giving him or her the inner strength to go on living.

In order to get your friend to see the brighter side of life, ask, "What was the best thing that ever happened to you?" Describe some of your own happy moments and draw your friend into talking about his or hers. Getting your friend to talk about happier times will be a reminder that things are not always bleak. We all need those reminders every now and then.

Most people who are thinking of suicide are suffering from a lot of guilt. If you think that might be what is troubling your friend, say something like, "Let's exchange stories. I'll tell you the worst thing I ever did and you tell me the worst thing you ever did." You might add, "Make it something you never told anyone else." I tried this with some adults and it was amazing. People started confessing things that they had done or that had happened to them when they were children or teenagers. Almost all the stories had to do with sex or stealing.

When the confession session was all over, people were laughing and acting strangely lighthearted. It seems as if the confession helped to free them of burdens of guilt they had carried around with them for years. Could it be that we were relieved because we all naturally comforted each other with words like, "Oh, that's not so terrible," or "I can imagine how you must have felt," or "That's a shame. I'm so sorry you had to go through that." (This last was said in response to a woman who told us that she had been sexually abused by her brother.)

So that the confession won't seem one-sided, you, too, should confess and let your friend console you. Then listen to your friend and do the same for him or her. If your friend believes in God, you can suggest talking to God about the guilt. Remind your friend that God forgives everything.

Another way to help your friend to change a gloomy view of the world to a more hopeful one is to recommend one of the many good books about positive thinking that are suggested in my bibliography—or this one. The two of you could read the book together, or you could ask your friend for an opinion of some passage that you've picked out ahead of time and think would be particularly helpful to him or her. You could even pretend you're doing a book report and need some help in explaining what the author is getting at—or you could just say you read the book and need to talk about it with somebody. By getting your friend involved in explaining positive thinking, you put the focus on ideas that are just what a depressed person needs to hear. Soon enough your friend will want to try them out to see if they could possibly work. And they do!

Another way to get your friend's mind off suicide is to divert it to something else.

– GETTING YOUR FRIEND'S MIND OFF SUICIDE –

Think of something your friend does well in and ask for help in that area. Be sure to act as if you *really need* help. For example, if your friend is a good swimmer, ask him or her to help you to learn to swim. If you're having trouble in a school subject your friend does well in, ask for help with that. And so forth. Then show a great appreciation for any help you get. Make your friend feel needed and important. Getting involved in helping you will get your friend not only to forget his or her own situation for a few hours, but to see that other people have problems, too.

Ask your friend to go somewhere with you—anywhere. It could be to a movie, to visit a cousin or another friend, shopping, or to see a school game. Tell your friend you really want to go but you hate to go alone and it would be a big favor if he or she went with you. By forcing your friend to move from point A to point B you will be stimulating different thought patterns. Sometimes a simple change of scene and some good company can do wonders.

Another way to get your friend's mind running on a

different track is to get that person involved in a physical activity. It's impossible to be depressed right after a fast-moving game, a good run, or a workout at the gym. The stimulation to the body and brain produces a natural high that drives away all depression for hours. Even that temporary relief can make all the difference, can break the depression cycle.

If all of your efforts seem to be failing, and you fear that your friend will do something drastic, you'll have to call in a professional.

– GETTING OUTSIDE HELP FOR YOUR FRIEND –

No matter what you have already done for your friend, you must inform a responsible adult about your friend's desire to commit suicide. Maybe you can talk to a teacher whom you trust. If the teacher doesn't know your friend, perhaps he can contact your friend's guidance counselor who could call your friend into the office on other business, and tactfully get into a discussion of what's really going on or, if that doesn't seem possible, can refer your friend to a psychologist who is trained to deal with potential suicides. If for some reason you can't go to a teacher or guidance counselor, don't give up. You still have an obligation to your friend to talk to an adult.

Maybe you could tell your parents and have them call your friend's parents. Often well-meaning parents have no idea how dangerously close their own child is to suicide. By alerting the parents, you give them a chance to help by getting their child into therapy—which is very often instrumental in saving the life of a would-be teenage suicide victim. Don't worry about making a fool of yourself. It's better to make a mistake and look like a jerk than to hold back and find out later that your friend is dead and you didn't do anything when there was still time to help. Don't take the chance. You're gambling with your friend's life.

If you've done all of the above but you still think your friend is about to commit suicide, use the suicide hotline in your town. You can get the number from information by asking for the emergency suicide hotline. If your friend won't call, then call yourself and hand the phone to your friend, or call and start explaining the situation and then hand the phone to your friend. Whatever you do, don't give up. Most suicides *can* be prevented.

If your friend refuses to talk to anyone else and begs you not to tell anyone, you must not feel obligated to honor such a request. Your first responsibility is to save your friend's life. Do not promise that you won't tell anyone. If you do make such a promise, it's okay to break it. In fact, you have an obligation to break it in order to save your friend's life.

No matter what happens, don't let yourself be the only one in on the situation. Tell a responsible adult (and make sure that adult is doing something to help your friend). It's too much of a burden on you to bear the responsibility of your friend's life or death alone.

What about someone who is just a casual acquaintance —someone you don't really know? Should you get involved?

– HELPING CASUAL ACQUAINTANCES AND NEAR STRANGERS –

Here's what happened to Melissa and Erin.

There's this girl in our social studies class and everyone is always talking about her and calling her a tramp. Melissa and I know how she feels because last year people were passing rumors about us and we felt so badly we wanted to die. So we wrote her this note, even though we're not really her friend or anything:

Dear Linda:
If you ever need a friend or anything, or if you ever want someone to talk to, please call us. We understand.

Love, Erin and Melissa

She wrote back this note:

Dear Erin and Melissa:
Thank you so much. It really makes me feel better. I appreciate your understanding. I feel like everyone is against me. I didn't think I could take it any more. I'll call you if I need to talk.

Love, Linda

You'd be amazed how much something like that can mean. A simple note, a kind word, an affectionate gesture at the right moment, can save someone's life. You may never even know how much good you did. For all Melissa and Erin know, Linda could have been found dead the next morning of an overdose if they hadn't taken the time to write that note and show their compassion. Don't hold back and say to yourself: "I'll just mind my own business. I have troubles enough of my own." Do something. Follow your better instincts.

No one is telling you to spend twenty-four hours a day thinking about how to save people. But when something pops up in your face, just take a moment to do the right thing. That's all that can be expected of you. A smile, a pat on the shoulder, a kind look, a word of encouragement, a word of defense for someone who is being picked on. That's all you have to do, and you will feel wonderful. In fact, you'll have given yourself one more reason for living.

Saying: *Five minutes of your time can give someone a whole lifetime.*

– EPILOGUE: REMINDERS –

1. You can't change the "hand" life has dealt you, but you can play it well (or badly).
2. Load the camera of your mind with success movies instead of failure movies.
3. If your looks aren't perfect, use your charm.
4. Program your mind with the "comeback reaction," so that every time you fail at something that triggers anger, anger is sublimated and converted to energy, and you use that energy to attain another goal. Albert Einstein failed his college entrance exams. I guess he got angry enough to convert early failure into ultimate success.
5. You were born for a reason. Find out what it is and do it.

6. Use your subconscious mind to help you to zigzag your way toward your goal.

7. You'll get all the love you need if you make the first move. People are starving for your love.

8. Everyone will get what's coming to him or her. It's not your job to deliver it.

9. Build a good reputation with yourself by doing what you believe is right.

10. Don't let anyone else make you feel guilty.

11. Don't give in to fear. Beat it back.

12. If someone doesn't like you, that's their problem. Make sure you like yourself, and plenty of other people will, too.

13. If your parent rejects you, look for another adult to love and accept you. If you look, you'll find.

14. Everyone has problems. You're not alone. Don't be fooled by appearances.

15. You can make yourself lucky. Expect good luck and you'll get it.

16. You can move mountains. Remember the woman who lifted the 700-pound truck?

17. If the pressure gets to be too much, "shrug it off."

18. You *can* do it. Ever hear of the man who didn't know he couldn't and did?

19. Never badmouth yourself even in fun: Your subconscious mind can't take a joke.

20. When someone "kisses and tells," remember, if it's not on film, NOTHING HAPPENED.

21. Love is wonderful, but it's not worth dying for. If at first you don't succeed, then try again—and again. It keeps on getting better with practice.

22. Give yourself permission to mourn your tragedies. If you mourn fully now, you'll live fully later.

23. Watch for "Amazing Grace" to surface in your own life.

24. Use your mind and your will to kick the habit that's dragging you down. And if they're not enough, get outside help.
25. Get high on life, not drugs.
26. Life is as unpredictable as flying in combat. So don't give up—help is on the way.
27. You have the power to save another person's life. A simple word or gesture from you can make all the difference.
28. Keep your promises—to yourself, to others, and to life.

– REVIEW OF SAYINGS –

Here is a list of the sayings at the end of each chapter. Use them to remind you of the main point of each chapter. Pick out your favorites and post them somewhere to remind you and to inspire you. You might find yourself quoting them to friends at the appropriate time.

1. Let's get with the program!
2. Dare to be yourself!
3. He who does not have a dog to hunt with must use a cat!
4. Turn bad anger into good energy!
5. There's a whole lot of Karma goin' round!
6. Don't claim it!
7. You can't win 'em all, but you can win some!
8. I believe. I believe. I believe!
9. This too shall pass!
10. Another love *will* come along!
11. In the long run!
12. Amazing Grace!

13. Break the habit before it breaks you!
14. I have promises to keep!
15. Five minutes of your time can give someone a whole lifetime!

– BIBLIOGRAPHY –

Self-help Books

Bristol, Claude M. *The Magic of Believing*. New York: Pocket Books, 1948.

Girodo, Dr. Michael. *Shy? You Don't Have to Be*. New York: Pocket Books, 1978.

Hill, Napoleon. *Think & Grow Rich*. New York: Fawcett Crest, 1960.

Hoke, James H. *I Would If I Could and I Can*. New York: Berkley Books, 1980.

Kassorla, Dr. Irene. *Go For It!* New York: Dell Publishing Co. Inc., 1984.

Litvak, Stuart B. *Use Your Head*. New Jersey: Prentice Hall, 1982.

Peale, Norman Vincent. *The Power of Positive Thinking*. New York: Ballantine Books, 1965.

Peale, Norman Vincent. *The True Joy of Positive Thinking*. New York: Ballantine Books, 1984.

Schwartz, David. *The Magic of Thinking Big*. New York: Simon & Schuster, 1959.

Vedral, Joyce L., Ph.D. *I Dare You*. New York: Ballantine Books, 1983.

Vedral, Joyce, L., Ph.D. *My Parents Are Driving Me Crazy*. New York: Ballantine Books, 1986.

Psychology and Psychological Self-help Books

Adler, Alfred. *What Life Should Mean to You*. New York: G. P. Putnam's Sons, Perigree Books, 1931.

Jung, Carl G. *Memories, Dreams, Reflections*. Aneliea Jaffe, ed. Richard and Clara Winston, trans. New York: Random House, Vintage Books, 1961.

Jung, Carl G. *Syncronicity*. New Jersey: Princeton University Press, 1973.

Maltz, Maxwell, M.D., F.I.C.S. *Psychocybernetics*. Englewood Cliffs, New Jersey: Prentice Hall, 1960.

Peck, Scott M., M.D. *The Road Less Traveled*. New York: Simon & Schuster, 1978.

Viscott, David, M.D. *Risking*. New York: Simon & Schuster, 1977.

Weinberg, Dr. George. *Self Creation*. New York: St. Martin's Press, 1978.

Wilson, Donald L., M.D. *Total Mind Power*. New York: Berkley Books, 1978.

Wood, Paul E., M.D. *How to Get Yourself to Do What You Want to Do*. Englewood Cliffs, New Jersey: Prentice Hall, 1981.

Suicide and Depression

Gordon, Sol. *When Living Hurts*. New York: Union of American Hebrew Congregation, 1985.

Hazleton, Lesley. *The Right to Feel Bad*. New York: Ballantine Books, 1984.

Kiev, Ari, M.D. *Riding Through the Hassles, Snags and Funks*. New York: E.P. Dutton, 1980.

Klagsbrun, Francine. *Too Young to Die*. New York: Pocket Books, 1981.

McCoy, Kathleen. *Coping With Teenage Depression*. New York: New American Library, 1982.

Myers, Irma and Arthur Myers. *Why You Feel Down and What You Can do About it*. New York: Charles Scribner & Sons, 1982.

Religions and Philosophy

Alport, Gordon W. *The Individual and His Religion*. New York: Macmillan Publishing Co. 1950.

The Book. Tyndale House Publishers, Inc. Wheaton, Illinois, 1984. (This is a very modern, simple translation of the Bible. Easy reading compared to most other translations.)

Schuller, Robert. *The Be Happy Attitudes*. Texas: Word Inc. 1985.

Biographies and Auto-Biographies

Ali, Muhammad. *The Greatest*. New York: Random House, 1975.

Eisenhower, Dwight D. *At Ease*. New York: Doubleday & Company, 1967.

Iacocca, Lee with William Novak. *Iacocca*. New York: Bantam Books, 1984.

Yeager, Chuck and Leo Janis. *Yeager*. New York: Bantam Books, 1985.

Sex and Sexuality

Coles, Robert & Geoffrey Stokes. *Sex and the American Teenager*. New York: Rolling Stone Press, 1985.

Nonkin, Lesley Jane. *I Wish My Parents Understood: A Report on the Teenage Female*. New York: Freundlich Books, 1985.

Westheimer, Dr. Ruth and Dr. Nathan Kravetz. *First Love*. New York: Warner Books, 1985.

Bodybuilding

Hatfield, Fredrich C., Ph.D. *Bodybuilding. A Scientific Approach*. Chicago: Contemporary Books Inc., 1985.

Sprague, Ken and Bill Reynolds. *The Gold's Gym Book of Bodybuilding*. Chicago: Contemporary Books Inc., 1983.

Vedral, Joyce, Ph.D. *Now or Never*. New York: Warner Books, Inc., 1986.

Vocabulary and Books About Words

Ciardi, John. *A Browser's Dictionary: A Compendium of Curious Expressions & Intriguing Facts*. New York: Harper & Row, 1980.

Hunsberger, Moyer I. *The Quintessential Dictionary*. New York: Warner Books, 1978.

Levine, Harold. *Vocabulary for the College Bound Student*. New York: Amsco School Publications, 1983.

Excellent Information on Alcohol and Drugs

O'Brien, Robert and Morris Chafetz, M.D. *The Encyclopedia of Alcoholism*. New York: Facts on File Publications, 1982.

O'Brien, Robert O. and Sidney Cohen, M.D. *The Encyclopedia of Drug Abuse*. New York: Facts on File Publications Inc., 1984.

Fiction Related to Depression and Suicide

Green, Hannah. *I Never Promised You a Rose Garden*. New York: Holt, Rinehart Winston, 1964.

Guest, Judith, *Ordinary People*. New York: Penguin, 1982.

Plath, Sylvia. *The Bell Jar*. New York: Bantam Books, 1975.

– Index –

– ABOUT THE AUTHOR –

Joyce Vedral, a Ph.D. in English Literature, has been involved with the problems of young adults for the past twenty years. She has taught English at Julia Richman High School and Pace University in New York City. But her real expertise in dealing with the problems and concerns of teenagers comes, perhaps more than anything, from dealing with her fifteen-year-old daughter and her teenage friends.

Joyce has written for *Parents* magazine, *Seventeen* magazine and is a regular contributor to several bodybuilding magazines, amongst them *Shape, Female Bodybuilding* and *Muscle* and *Fitness*.

Her other teen self-help books, *I Dare You* and *My Parents Are Driving Me Crazy*, were selected by the American Library Association as one of the best books of the year for teens.

She is also the author of *Now or Never*, a fitness book for women, and is co-author of several other fitness books.

Joyce enjoys lecturing to live audiences. When asked why she writes for teenagers, Joyce says: "I write for them because I remember the pain. I know what it is to be misunderstood, to feel rejected, to suspect I was the only one in the world to feel this way and to wonder if I were normal. So I write for teenagers because I want to make it a little easier for them to get through the tough years and to emerge into the clear sailing time, then the real fun begins."